HYPNOSTAMP

Uncovering the Healing Power of Postage Stamps

George Toth, LCSW-R

HYPNOSTAMP
UNCOVERING THE HEALING POWER OF POSTAGE STAMPS

iUniverse books may be ordered through booksellers or by contacting:

iUniverse
1663 Liberty Drive
Bloomington, IN 47403
www.iuniverse.com
844-349-9409

ISBN: 978-1-6632-2202-2 (sc)
ISBN: 978-1-6632-4152-8 (hc)
ISBN: 978-1-6632-1943-5 (e)

Library of Congress Control Number: 2023902297

Print information available on the last page.

iUniverse rev. date: 05/01/2023

To my wife, Diana Marie, for all of her love and support.

Also by George Toth:

Marble Mindfullness: Unlock Your Family's Hidden Messages

How to Hypnotize Your Grandchildren: Easy, Quick, and Fun Ways to Influence the Children in Your Life

Seashell Therapy: Discover the Healing Power of the Sea

CONTENTS

LIST OF IMAGES

ACKNOWLEDGMENT

I express gratitude to my wife, Diana Marie, for her support and encouragement in developing this book as a positive theraputic tool and balancing energy source.

I thank my daughter, Tracy Gillespie, for implementing the idea of using US stamp number 5,100 of Jaime Escalante (high school calculus teacher) from *Scott Standard Catalogue of Postage Stamps* as motivation and inspiration for her mathematics colleagues and students.

I express thanks to my grandchildren, Savannah Skye Fahrbach and Cash Christopher Fahrbach, for their support with the technology needed to write this book.

Thank you to the staff of the American Philatelic Society Research Library for your consultation support.

Thank you, Mystic Stamp Company, for your stamp catalog information and stamp promotional ideas.

INTRODUCTION

Welcome to the world of *Hypnostamp*. It is likely that postage stamps are generally not on most people's minds, unless they need one to place on an envelope to send it through the mail. That mindset can change forever after reading this book. It is just the beginning for an additionl awareness of life on earth. Stamps have been a common and familiar thread woven in or around almost all aspects of my life, including my childhood, education, marriage, family, career, army service, and residences around the world. Although I have spent many decades as a collector and non-collector of stamps, I was always mindful of the amazing learning values inherent in the nature of postage stamps. If you collect postage stamps, you are officially called a *philatelist* or, more commonly, a stamp collector.

Let it be known that this book is not actually about collecting stamps. It is about having an interest in and knowledge of postage stamps, therefore uncovering how stamps are used as windows and backstories to the world. Further, postage stamps can be used as conduits for reducing stress and healing. As a professional social worker and psychotherapist, it dawned on me that you can improve your life with postage stamps. They can be a tool for wellness and feeling better. This was my primary reason for writing this book. I wanted to share and tout this wonderful feeling and discovery. This book will be of great interest and benefit for everyone, non-collectors and collectors alike. It is also considered a self-help healing book for anyone and considered a go-to book for those in the holistic healing profession.

You will learn that there are so many benefits gained from being interested in postage stamps that it boggles the mind. As you begin to learn about postage stamps, it will soon be apparent that a paradox exists in philately. On one hand, stamp collecting offers many participants mental stimulation and challenges. On the other hand, it offers others the power of relaxation and calmness. These benefits are felt to varying degrees in each person. Since all people are different, not everyone can find stimulation and challenge along with relaxation and calmness. However, many collectors are able to combine these apparently contradictory benefits, therefore achieving both stimulation and relaxation. This characteristic of philately was probably best summed up by the late founder and editor of *Stamps*, Harry Linquest, when he wrote the following:

> There is something peculiarly soothing to the mind and calming to the nerves in stamp collecting. No matter how inescapable may be the trouble that is weighing him down, the collector will find temporary forgetfulness in his stamp albums. Then after an hour or two with his stamps, when he returns to his problem, it is with a refreshed mind and outlook; he often finds that the old enigma has a solution after all, which his tired mind, running in circles, had not been able to discover. The hobby of stamp collecting not only heals and refreshes the tired mind, but becomes a healthy stimulant to the idle mind. The reason that the burdened mind is rested during a session with stamps is that the brain is quickened into other avenues of thought by many fascinating subjects they suggest. These same qualities stir the mind that has been dulled by inaction, as sometimes happens to our retired folk, or guide into worthwhile activity the eager mind of youth. (Holland 2020, 178)

By reading *Hypnostamp*, you will learn that postage stamps are hypnotic. I have actually been self-hypnotized since about the age of eight, when my older cousin first gave me an album and some stamps. After examining those stamps and learning what they represented and how they were used, I was on my way to a greater awareness of the world. Little did I know, I would develop an immediate and lifelong interest in the knowledge of postage stamps. Therefore, I was introduced to a new and higher state of mind for the rest of my life. I find it amazing that now, after many decades and differing levels of interest, I have been reawakened to the great positive energy that stamps contain. I am only now developing and using this energy in my profession as a clinical social worker and psychotherapist. You, too, will learn that stamps can be so powerful that people are often hypnotized by the mere thought of one.

One of the best examples of showing the therapeutic value of stamp collecting is cited in the life of the late president Franklin D. Roosevelt. He often turned to his stamp albums to unwind from the cares of office and take his mind from the pain that attacked his body as a result of the infantile paralysis he suffered as a young man. The importance of stamp collecting to President Roosevelt has been recorded by Harley Williams in his book *The Conquest of Fear*:

> [Roosevelt] had a remarkable faculty of relaxation. His stamp collection, a hobby began at the age of eight, was now caried on, and no U. S. issue went lacking his personal approval. Indeed, the President carried books of stamps to all his international conferences, and loved to bargain for specimens, ten dollars being his upper limit.

> As he used to watch his patient, sitting perfectly carefree, while he examined his blues and greens, it came to Dr. McIntyre [Roosevelt's physician]that a treatise could be written about the healing effect of such hobbies. Around this man in the White House, who was absorbed in philately each night before going to bed, the storm raged as it had never done even around Woodrow Wilson … dignified Americans declared that their President should be certified insane … he faced his enemies with the same outward composure as he moved his paralyzed legs. Upon such a regimen of severe mental labor, diet, massage, swimming and stamp collecting, the President took his first four-year term in his stride. (Williams 1952, 227–228)

Monaco issued a commemorative stamp in 1947, honoring President Roosevelt's stamp collecting activity. It was number C16 in the *Scott Standard Catalogue of Postage Stamps*. The stamp also shows a close-up of the famous six-finger design mistake on his left hand (see figure 1).

Figure 1: Monaco Scott # C16 Franklin D. Roosevelt, 1947.
Enlargement of Roosevelt's left hand showing 6 fingers.

4

The therapeutic value of stamp collecting felt by President Roosevelt has also been attested to by his son, James Roosevelt, in the forward he wrote for the book *Eleanor and Franklin D. Roosevelt Stamps of the World* by Philip Silver and Jan Bart. He wrote,

> I am delighted with the fine effort of Phil Silver and Jan Bart in their book, and I am sure it will bring great joy to many stamp collectors. Further I hope that it will be a reminder of how stamp collecting as a hobby can be turned into not only a part-time occupation—as it was in the case of my father—but therapy as well, better than any doctor could have prescribed. (Silver and Bart 1965)

You will find that postage stamps can heal the mind, body, and soul. They will inspire you. Postage stamps will help you maintain both the physical and mental wellness for balance in your state of life. These powerful thoughts and ideas about energy, balance, and healing will be demonstrated over and over again in this book. You will learn about yourself and about your personality characteristics and traits. You may increase your attention to detail, creativity, perseverance, organizational skills, linguistic proficiency, negotiation skills, decision-making abilities, independence, coordination, sense of responsibility, honesty, fairness, and character.

In order to gain a better perspective about how the healing and energy powers are attributed to postage stamps and how they and other positive traits are transferred into your life, I have organized this book into chapters. Chapter 1 will briefly discuss the beginnings of stamps, outlining when, how, and why stamps were used and including the development and nature of postal history.

In chapter 2, you will widen your scope and learn how stamps may influence and improve your life. You will also learn how stamps will eventually affect the way you think, feel, and behave. Stamps will help improve your memory and concentration. You may be able to think more clearly or become more emotionally calm and relaxed. In fact, you will experience the domino effect. When one positive change takes place in your life, other positive changes will occur. When you begin to feel better about yourself, you project a more powerful sense of confidence, strength, and stature. When this occurs, the new you may attract more people, ideas, and influences into your life. Be ready for others to begin seeing you in a healthier and more positive mode, opening up multiple ways of contributing to your life, family, friends, and community.

Stamps will also educate you. In chapter 3, you will learn about the people, geography, art, and history of the country that you live in. You will also greatly expand your knowledge of science, language, mathematics, medicine, literature, architecture, outer space, and the universe. The stamp organization called the American Topical Association (ATA) has identified over 2,500 separate topic areas of stamp and human being interest. New areas continue to be identified.

In chapter 4, you will learn about some postage stamp rarities, stamp errors, stamp oddities, and stamp special issues and effects. These will intrigue you and may affect your conscious and subconscious feelings. You will also learn that just as each postage stamp has a unique, distinguishable characteristic, each person on earth has a unique, identifiable characteristic. No two stamps or no two people are alike. We are often drawn to certain stamps for multiple reasons, including topic, color, value, country, size, and artwork. When placed in a hypnotic state, humans may become more capable of gaining insight into their own behavior and problem-solving abilities by selecting certain types of stamps subconsciously. Postage stamps may have differences such as country, use, date of issue, topic, design, color, cancelation, perforation grade, condition, denomination, language, and provenance. A stamp or stamps personally selected by an individual may provide insights into their own personality, characteristics, and behaviors. These insights may prove useful in making positive changes.

This is a testimony as to how postage stamps have the power to be a conduit in the human therapeutic healing process. Read this book, and discover how to uncover your own areas of personal positive change. Actual methods of how to use several unique techniques in the hypnotic process will be shown in chapter 5, including hypnosis, self-hypnosis, and visual imagery. Chapter 6 will offer case instances from my private psychotherapy practice. These will be inspiring.

Chapter 7 will train you on how to use postage stamp visual imagery scripts to complement more traditional treatment therapies. Chapter 8 will offer special exercises with actual postage stamps. Chapter 9 will show how several postage stamp schemes may reduce general stress and anxiety.

After reading *Hypnostamp: Uncovering the Healing Power of Postage Stamps*, you will immediately become more mindful of the power and energy available in stamps. You will be motivated to harness these attributes and concepts in order to improve all aspects of your life. You will have access to an amazing tool for the reduction of stress and anxiety. You will be more knowledgeable about the world.

This book will give you the tools to have a positive effect upon the way you think, feel, and behave. You will have increased concentration and self-confidence. You will be happier and have more fun. Stamps can be the healing window for the rest of your life. As you get involved with this book, postage stamps will touch, influence, and improve all aspects of your life. Be ready to attract new positive responses from the people around you. Again, welcome to the world of *Hypnostamp*. Be ready to be the new you.

1

....

When and Why Postage Stamps
Came into Existance

The first postage stamp, called the Penny Black, was issued by Great Britain in 1840. It pictured an engraving of Queen Victoria (see figure 2).

Figure 2: Great Britain Scott # 1 Penny Black, 1840.

Penny Blacks were issued in nonperforated sheets of one hundred stamps that had to be separated with scissors or knives. A different letter of the alphabet was located in each lower corner of the stamp to identify its position on the sheet, therefore making no two stamps alike. These stamps were called definitive issues or regular issues and were sold at post offices, remaining in use for long periods of time.

There was an increasing need to send documents and written messages to people locally and internationally. The cost per stamp in Great Britain was one English penny. Stamps were attached to envelopes with glue and mailed. Letter size, weight, distance, transportation method, and delivery time became factors in cost. Further, insurance, safety, and special handling issues became important. The popularity with this stamp and method of payment for letter delivery was accepted and quickly grew in many countries around the world.

In 1847, the first stamp was issued in the United States. It had an engraving of Benjamin Franklin (the first United States Postmaster) and showed the words "post office" on the top of the stamp and "five cents" on the bottom. Today, it is known as Scott #1. The ten-cent George Washington stamp known as Scott #2 was also issued at the same time, creating the first issue set (see figure 3).

Figure 3: US Scott # 1 Benjamin Franklin and US Scott # 2 George Washington, 1847.

These stamps were also not perforated.

In later years, postage stamps were issued to commemorate events, historical milestones, activities, or locations. With the beginning of commemoratives, it was apparent that each stamp had a story to tell about history and culture. This factor became a vehicle in bringing our rich national heritage to life. It opened the doors of American life and relationships to other ideas, people, and places. A valuable educational path was created and developed, letting people who were interested in collecting stamps learn about world history and significant global events.

Over the years, the world has honored men, women, and events that make nations great. Thousands of people were highlighted for their contributions to life and society. Stamps are miniature masterpieces of design that depict a host of fascinating subjects. They have become one of earth's most effective mediums of cultural exchange. Notable people were collectors, including queens, kings, and heads of governments, industries, arts, sciences, and sports. They became knowledgeable of the magic and power of postage stamps. Popular areas of interest to collectors identified by the American Topical Association (ATA) include:

- language
- music
- dance
- medicine
- mathematics
- movie stars
- baseball
- social studies
- culture
- space
- animals
- recreation
- sports
- politics

These topics may become more specific or more general as desired. They are constantly evolving and moving as the world and collectors change. For example, the current effects of the COVID-19 virus on world health, economics, science, and politics will influence what future stamps are issued. Your knowledge of past, present, and future stamps will add to your understanding and feelings about your surroundings and life decisions. I remember the first issue of postage stamps produced by the United Nations in 1951. These stamps were very interesting because you could only purchase them from the United Nations in New York City. They also commemorated worldwide issues. These stamps could only be used when mailed from the United Nations post office. They were not valid for postage use anywhere in the United States or any country in the world. My interest in these stamps increased because those characteristics made the stamps special and unusual. Further, they commemorated many of the United Nation's lofty global goals, such as maintaining international security, providing humanitarian assistance to those in need, protecting human rights, and upholding universal law. I felt especially gratified and awestruck by the stamps from the World Health Organization (WHO), first issued in 1956 (see figure 4).

Figure 4: United Nations Scott # 43 World Health Organization and
United Nations Scott # 44 World Health Organization, 1956.

These stamps commemorated the goal of attaining the highest possible level of health for all people in the world. I felt mesmerized by the benevolent and moral improvements possible in this world, represented by this stamp and other United Nations stamps.

Another example of international collaboration was the recent establishment of the US Space Corps. The cooperation was evident with stamps issued by the Apollo-Soyuz Space Venture (see figure 5).

Figure 5: US Scott # 1569 and US Scott # 1570, 1956.

What a wonderful feeling to realize that different countries can work together on common goals. It is also a good sensation to realize the interconnectivity between stamps, countries, feelings, and wellness.

2

. . . .

How Stamps May Improve and Influence Your Life

Each stamp issued brings to life people, countries, and ways to live nationally and internationally. Over the years, thousands of stamps have presented a comprehensive portrayal of the world and life past, present, and future. Additionally, stamps are miniature masterpieces of art and design that depict a host of fascinating subjects. Postage stamps provide the worlds' most effective medium of cultural exchange.

A widely accepted, organized stamp listing was needed and developed by the Scott Publishing Company. This all-inclusive catalog is aimed to serve the educational and commercial needs of collectors and dealers. It sets the standard for philatelic information and products, helping collectors identify, value, organize, and present their collections. It provides detailed information on catalog values, grade, and condition through actual publication. Further, this catalog provides basic stamp information, including details on plates, printings, papers, separations, gums, luminescence, postal markings, and general glossaries. The Scott Catalogue assigns a stamp number (known as the Scott Catalogue number) for each stamp issued in the world. Several different catalogs of the United States and other stamp-issuing countries are also available.

By learning about postage stamps, you will also unearth magical pathways to personal development. Your knowledge of the world will improve in all areas. A domino effect will take place, and you will be able to expand your interests and creativity. You will think more clearly, increase your concentration, feel more confident, and improve your awareness. You will become more relaxed and reduce your stress. In fact, you will learn how to develop a tool box of stress reduction and antianxiety methods to use for the rest of your life. You will greatly expand your interests, reason more clearly, increase your attentiveness, and improve your cognizance of the world around you.

You can use your mind to help affect the change you want in your life. You can imagine or reimagine anything. Postage stamps are so diverse and wide ranging in subject matter, which can be meaningful to you. You can visualize the concept with this statement: postage stamps and hypnosis equal wellness. Whatever the issue, you can visulize the concept through a postage stamp and make it come to life. There are no limits to your imagination, and there are seemingly unlimited stamps and interest areas. This amazing opportunity is available to you simply by putting your mind to work and adding stamps.

Self-hypnosis, visual imagery, and other imaginative techniques will be explored later in this book. For example, certain stamps may serve as symbols of healing and wellness. Depending on the individuals presenting issues, these might be stamps representing heros, water, flowers, trees, paintings, art, celebrities, music, shells, sports, religious themes, healing, treatment, earth, or medicine. You will see how some of these themes are used in chapter 6 with specific case examples. The key is to be aware of your or the individual's concerns and to be creative with which specific stamps may serve as channels for healing. Some stamps may be personal, and some may be general to the healing process. It is also possible that you may not be aware of why you feel better or more in balance and, therefore, not attribute possitive changes in feelings to stamps.

Many people develop passions and excitement when connecting with stamps. I believe that stamps can act as a gyroscope in your life. You always have an awareness of stamps that may appeal to you for different reasons. For example, they may serve as conscious or subconscious reminders of positive memories, happy times, success, hopes, dreams, and goals. Like a gyroscope, this will maintain and keep your balance in life forever. You will gain the constructive attributes delineated in this book.

I became more aware of the magic and hypnotic healing power of stamps with Hawaiian stamps. When Captain James Cook of the British Navy came upon the Hawaiian Islands in 1778, they were a kingdom under the rule of King Kamehameha. The islands were an independent kingdom until 1893, when the sovereign, Queen Liliuokalani, was deposed. Many American missionaries have settled there since. At the request of the people, Hawaii was formally annexed as a US territory in 1898. US postage stamps were first used in 1900. In 1959, Hawaii became the fiftieth US state. It's interesting that the stamps of

Hawaii honor various kings and queens and other royal figures. My interest in Hawaiian stamps has increased over the years because my birth country is the United States. My wife grew up in Hawaii, and I have visited several times. You could say that I was hypnotized by my wife and by learning about Hawaii and its stamps.

I immediately became fascinated by many of Hawaii's first stamps, issued when it was considered an independent kingdom. The first four stamps issued in 1851 and 1852 are known throughout the world as the extremely rare "missionaries." They are worth thousands of dollars each, depending on their condition. Most of these early stamps have minor damage and have been skillfully repaired over the years. Stamps issued from 1853 to 1863 are also extremely rare and often have minor damage. I felt fortunate to be able to collect a few of these antique Hawaiian stamps. I didn't mind having minor faults on them. They were still attractive because of their rare status and lower cost. I was thrilled to place them in my collection.

Hawaii Scott #5 was issued in 1853. It depicts King Kamehameha (see figure 6).

Figure 6: Hawaii Scott # 5 King Kamehameha This stamp has a small 1 centimeter tear on the upper right side, affecting the market value, 1853.

Although the catalog value of this rare stamp is $1,900, the true market value is based on the stamp condition and what a collector is willing to pay for it. My stamp has a small, one-centimeter tear in the right upper side. Otherwise it looks clean and attractive for its age. Can you find one in perfect condition or any other condition? What would you be willing to pay for it?

Hawaii Scott #10s and #11s were both issued in 1868 and depicted King Kamehameha. These stamps were official reprints. Some were overprinted with the word *speciman* (see figures 7 and 8).

Figure 7: Hawaii Scott 10s King Kamehameha SPECIMAN, 1868.

Figure 8: Hawaii Scott # 11s King Kamehameha SPECIMAN, 1868. This stamp was never placed in use, but it was sold at the Honolulu post office.

They were never placed in use, but stamps with and without the overprint were sold at face value at the Honolulu post office.

My Hawaii Scott #6 is a forgery with nice cancellation (see figure 9).

Figure 9: Hawaii Scott # 6 King Kamehameha III FORGERY . If original, this stamp would now have a catalogue value of $1,700.00.

If original, this stamp would now have a catalog value of $1,700. Hawaii Scott #28 was issued 1861–1863 on vertically laid paper and depicted King David Kalakua (see figure 10).

Figure 10: Hawaii Scott # 28 King (Elua Kenta) David Kalakua , 1861–1863. This stamp was printed on vertically laid paper, also known as Batonne. It has watermark lines deliberately added in the papermaking process and intended as a guide for handwriting.

Hawaii Scott #29s were issued in 1889. This stamp is of King David Kalakua, who was the last ruling king and wrote Hawaii's state song. It was not issued for postal purposes, although cancelled examples are known. It was sold only at the Honolulu post office. First it was sold without overprint. Later the word *cancelled* was added (see figure 11).

Figure 11: Hawaii Scott # 29s (51) King Kamehameha IV 1889 CANCELLED. This stamp was not issued for postal purposes and sold at the Honolulu post office. The word CANCELLED was later added.

As you can see, the detailed information for these old stamps is incredible. This is just a small example of how intricate and minute stamp descriptions can be within the same printed example. Colors; engraving and plate differences; types of paper, grills, and ink; print quality and quantity; and current condition all make a difference in value and desirability. One can easily get lost or absorbed within these details, becoming hypnotized. For example, you can get so engrossed in the minute details of stamp identification that life around you will be blocked from your conscious mind. Your total focus will be concerned with the stamp. You can automatically block everything else out, including sound, sight, and outside stimuli. When you come out of this trance-like state, you may feel better and well rested. Your brain has been given a break from any normal and routine duties. This is just the beginning.

I was also fascinated by stamps from the United Nations. The first United Nations stamps were issued in 1951. The world headquarters for the United Nations was established in New York City. I was lucky enough to live about twenty miles from New York City, in suburban New Jersey, and I remember making several bus and car trips to the United Nations to buy stamps from their post office at face value. It was always exciting to walk from the Port of Authority Bus Terminal, down Forty-Second Street, and to the United Nations building. I was always eager and looked forward to finding out what new stamps were available for purchase. Through these stamps, I learned about various countries and world issues while helping commemorate health, hunger, economic, science, and quality of life. Specific issues included:

- the Universal Postal Union
- technical assistance
- human rights
- food and agriculture
- the International Labor Organization
- United Nations Day
- Human Rights Day
- the International Telecommunication Union
- the World Health Organization
- the General Assembly
- the World Meteorological Organization
- the United Nations Emergency Force
- the Security Council
- atomic energy

- Central Hall Westminster
- Flushing Meadows
- the Economic Commission for Europe
- the Trusteeship Counsel
- World Refugee Year
- the Palais de Chaillot
- the Economic Commission for Asia
- the World Forestry Congress
- the International Bank for Reconstruction and Development
- the International Court of Justice
- the International Monetary Fund
- the Economic Commission for Latin America
- the United Nations Children's Fund
- the Economic Commission for Africa

All stamps were issued from the United Nations and could only be used for mailing letters and packages from there. I usually collected inscription blocks. Two stamps I collected were Scott UN #17 and #18, both issued in 1953 (see figure 12).

Figure 12: United Nations Offices in New York Scott # 17 and
18 Universal Postal Union First Day Cover 1953

The Ryukyu Islands were part of Japan until American forces occupied them in 1945. The islands reverted back to Japan in 1972. During the Vietnam War, I was an active-duty soldier in the US Army, stationed in Okinawa in the Ryukyu Islands. My curiosity in stamps continued at that time. It was interesting to go to the town's local post office and purchase stamps. To my surprise, I later found out that I had bought stamps the "wrong way." I purchased stamps in plate blocks of four, just as I had collected them in the United States. Most collectors in Okinawa acquired stamps as singles or in sheets of ten. I did not collect sheets of stamps because I thought they were composed of one hundred stamps each, therefore too large, cumbersome, and expensive to obtain. When I asked for plate blocks in Okinawa, the postal clerk didn't know what I was talking about. The clerk was reluctant to sell me a block of four. They didn't understand why I would break up a sheet of ten just to get four stamps. I quickly learned that different countries may have different ways of collecting and issuing stamps. I also obtained some first day covers (see figure 13).

Figure 13: Ryukyu Islands (Okinawa) Scott #43 Sheet of 10, Tenth Anniversary of First Stamp, 1958.

First day covers are special cached envelopes mailed on the stamp's first day of issue and postmarked "first day of issue," along with the date and city of origination. First day covers in Okinawa were collected in the same way as those sold in the United States and other countries.

From 930 to 1264, Iceland was an independent republic. A treaty then recognized the king of Norway. In 1914, Norway separated from Denmark, and Iceland remained under the rule of Danish Kings. The 1918 Act of Union of the King connected Iceland with Denmark in some areas. The first stamp issued by Iceland was in 1878 and identified as Scott #1. I attended a conference in Iceland. In addition to presenting a paper at the International Conference for the Advancement of Clinical Social Work, I enjoyed touring the capital city and the volcanic landscape as well as viewing hot springs, geysers, and waterfalls. Of special note was experiencing the Blue Lagune, the site of the famous therapeutic and healing natural volcanic hot springs and mud baths. While there, I added Scott #250 and #438 to my collection, as examples of the volcanic landscapes (see figure 14).

Figure 14: Island Scott # 1 First Issue of the Country, 1873, Iceland Scott # 250
Helka Volcano, 1947, and Iceland Scott # 438 Herdubreid Mountain, 1972.

According to the Scott Catalogue, the first stamp of Germany was issued in 1872 (see figure 15).

Figure 15: Germany Scott # 1 German Empire Imperial Eagle. 1872.

I lived in Germany for five years as a US employee of the Department of the Army. I lived in the small village of Osterholz-Scharmbeck. I didn't experience much involvement with stamps at that time, but I did go to antique flea markets. Instead of postage stamps, I found other types of collectibles. These included movie star stickers, cigar bands, sports stickers, antique music boxes, old clocks, and aged furniture. My recently acquired German Empire Scott #1 represents the idea of obtaining the first stamp issued in countries that I have visited or that have touched my life in significant ways.

Hungary is a country in central Europe. Prior to World War II, it was comprised of the Austro-Hungarian Empire. Since my ancestors are of Hungarian decent, I was always interested in Hungarian stamps. My grandparents came to the United States from Hungary in the 1890s. My mother and father were born in the United States, but both were able to speak and understand Hungarian. My father was a butcher and a grocer, owning a store in Garfield, New Jersey. He specialized in making Hungarian kolbasa. My mother spent much time in her kitchen, preparing Hungarian foods like stuffed cabbage and poppyseed cake. During the Hungarian revolution in 1956, our family sponsored a few relatives as they fled to the United States to live. Since I was a young stamp collector at the time, my parents tried to obtain stamps for me. I did get a few, mostly on mailed letters sent to my family. As a member of the Society of Philatelic Americans, I used their translation services to translate many letters from Hungarian to English. According to the letters, the main interest for my relatives at that time was to obtain medicine for survival that was unavailable in Europe.

The first Hungarian stamp, issued in 1872, was of Emperor Francis Joseph I. I also collected a Greek stamp that commemorates the third anniversary of the 1956 Hungarian Revolution. Both of these images are shown in figure 16.

Figure 16 : Scott # 1a Emperor Frances Joseph I , 1866 and Greece Scott 664–5 Prime Minster
Imere Nagy, commemorating the third anniversary of the Hungarian Revolution, 1959.

This uprising was a spontaneous, nationwide revolt against the Communist government of Hungary and its Soviet-imposed policies. The revolution lasted from October 23 to November 10, 1956. The revolution eventually failed to defeat the soviet domination. The Hungarian freedom fighters were terminated. Hungarian Prime Minister Imere Nagy was jailed and put to death.

I found a fascinating stamped envelope from the 1956 Hungarian revolutionary time period with my family's papers and records (see figure 17).

Figure 17: Envelope to "Mr. Gorge, who has a store on the corner of Division Ave, Garfield."

I only had the envelope with common stamps used by the Azores, no letter contents. The stamps were from Portugal. The envelope was interesting in that it was addressed to my father: "Mr. Gorge, who owns a store on the corner of Division Ave. Garfield, New Jersey, US America." I have no further information about this very fascinating piece of mail. More examination is needed. Can you think of explorable interest areas in your life that connect you to stamps or postal history? A few ideas might include:

- ethnic foods on stamps
- emperors, dictators, kings, queens, and presidents on stamps
- unusual postal markings and notations on envelopes
- ancestral connections on stamps
- medicine on stamps
- revolutions and war on stamps
- grandparents, mothers, and fathers on stamps
- Texas events on stamps
- India on stamps
- survival issues on stamps
- stamps issued around the world in 2005
- insects on stamps
- female basketball players on stamps
- dolls on stamps
- bridges on stamps
- toys on stamps

Life connections with postage stamps are important. They may provide feelings of grounding and stability over decades of life. They become part of a person's history, growing stronger as the years go by. One of the most significant times in my life was when I was a Boy Scout. I tried to live by the scout oath and law. The scout oath is "be prepared." The scout law is that "a scout is trustworthy, loyal, helpful, friendly, courteous, kind, obedient, thrifty, cheerful, brave, clean, and reverent." As I look back, it's interesting that the stamps that stand out and are important to me often have these themes. I remember brave, kind, helpful, and courteous. Stamps related to these themes seemed attractive and more interesting to me, probably on an unconscious level. I also remember the fun I had while working for the Scout's stamp-collecting merit badge. The merit badge requirements and stamps collected for the badge, gave me an informative introduction to the world.

The requirements included defining terms and supported what I needed to know to expand my interest and collection. They were printed in the Boy Scouts of America's *Handbook for Boys* in 1955. It's interesting to compare past and present stamp collecting and postal history techniques over the span of a decade or more. Do collecting methods differ from the past? Why or why not? The following tasks were required for the Boy Scout's stamp-collecting merit badge:

1. Mount and exhibit in a commercial album or album of your own making: (a) A collection of 750 or more different stamps from at least thirty countries: or (b) A collection of 150 or more different stamps from a single country or a group of closely related countries, or (c) A collection of 75 or more different stamps on some special subject such as birds, trees, great men, music, aviation etc. (Stamps may be from any number of countries) or (d) A collection of 200 or more items such as precanceled stamps, postage meters revenue stamps, covers, postal stationary, etc.
2. Demonstrate the use of the Standard Postage Stamp Catalogue, or a catalogue particularly related to your collection in requirement 1, to find at least five items selected by the Counselor.
3. Show stamps to support brief definitions of the following terms: perforation, roulette, cancelation, cover, mint stamp, coil stamp, overprint, surcharge, engraving, and a printing process other than engraving.
4. Exhibit one stamp in each of the following classifications and explain the purpose of each: regular postage, commemorative, semi postal, airmail, postage due, envelope, special delivery, precancel, and revenue.
5. Explain the meaning of good condition of a stamp and show one stamp that is well centered, fully perforated, clearly cancelled, clean and undamaged by tears or thin spots.
6. Demonstrate a knowledge of the following stamp collector tools: (a) Use a perforation gauge to determine, on a stamp supplied by the Counselor, the perforation measurement in accordance with the accepted standard. (b) Use a magnifying glass for careful examination of design and condition. (c) Use a watermark detector to show how a watermark may aid in identifying a stamp (d) Use stamp tongs and stamp hinges correctly in mounting a stamp in an album. (Pettit 1948, 518–519)

It's interesting to note that the Boy Scouts of America's *Handbook for Boys* merit requirements for stamp collecting were developed more than sixty years ago. Today, stamps are more advanced in production, design, quality, album design, mounting tools, and organization. The computer and photo-image productions have come into existence and advanced the nature of collecting, sales, marketing, and pleasure. Stamps that are more than one hundred years old are considered classic and antiques. I often enjoy viewing enlarged color images of stamps on my electronic device, rather than looking at the stamp itself. This is especially true for stamps with old engraved images, art, or insects. Take Scott #995 for example, which honored the Boy Scouts by commemorating the 40th Anniversary of Boy Scouts of America, 1950. (see figure 18).

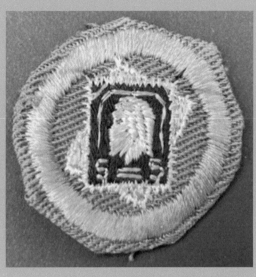

Figure 18: US Scott # 995 First Day Cover, commemorating
40th Anniversary of Boy Scouts of America, 1950.
Boy Scout Stamp Collecting merit badge.

Also included is an image of the stamp-collecting merit badge that was awarded at the time.

The therapeutic concepts within stamps can be expanded even further. Positive, stable, and curative qualities also stemmed from my years of volunteer service in activities. These activities included being the former president of the local Rotary and local Lions clubs; an American Red Cross volunteer; and a member of the American Legion, the Chamber of Commerce, the YMCA (Young Men's Christian Association), the Boys Clubs of America, the Catholic Youth Organization (CYO), and the Babe Ruth League. These organizations have been recognized by countries around the world, commemorating their values and goals. Many of these positive attributes have become imbedded in my mind. The stamps may serve as an ongoing conscious and subconscious reminder to maintain your life's balance and mental well-being.

3

The Relationship between
People and Stamps

By the end of the nineteenth century, it was possible to complete a collection of all the postage stamps issued in the world. However, after that time, so many stamps were being issued that it became necessary to specialize by country, location, design, subject, people, places, objects, events, or other characteristics. The American Topical Association (ATA) revealed the most popular topics for stamps in the United States:

- Americana
- art
- birds
- Christmas
- Europa
- famous people
- flags
- flowers
- Lions International
- maps
- marine life
- masonry
- medicine

- music
- paintings
- railroads
- the Red Cross
- religion
- Rotary International
- scouts
- ships
- space
- sports
- stamps

More specific themes may include:

- ambulances
- bearded men
- hats
- Hummel figurines (now appearing on ninety stamps)
- left-handed personalities
- Mathematic teachers
- monsters (i.e., demons, ghouls, werewolves, witches, and vampires)
- parlor games
- pirates
- puzzles
- science fiction (such as works of Edgar Allen Poe and Jules Verne)
- Winnie the Pooh (and other teddy bears)
- world wonders (i.e., Colossus of Rhodes, Babylon Hanging Gardens)

As you can imagine, each theme or topic can be explored by the collector in many creative ways. The ATA can supply members with checklists as aids in developing topical collections. Each topical check list contains a topic, country, date of issue, Scott number, and stamp description. An extremely popular topic on stamps is sports, specifically baseball (see figure 20).

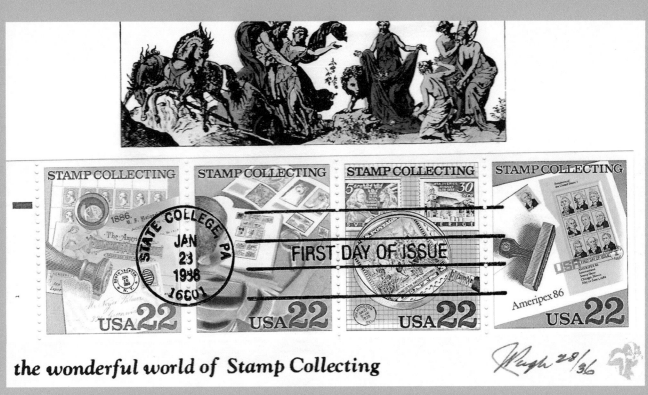

Figure 19: US Scott # 8603 The Wonderful World of Stamp Collecting Commemorative Booklet Pane 1986

Your collection could be further limited to one country. I was especially interested in baseball since I played the sport and collected baseball cards. Much like stamps, collecting baseball cards and many other sports cards became increasingly popular as a relaxing and hypnotic activity. Another relaxing topic is stamps on stamps or stamps comemorating stamp collecting (see figure 19).

Figure 20: US Scott # 4080–4083 Baseball Sluggers include Micky
Mantle, Mell Ott, Hank Greenberg, and Roy Campanella.

This is a very popular, global topic.

Imagine the power created by having an interest in collecting stamps on stamps or combining collecting stamps with your career, educational interests, beliefs, values, goals, avocation, future plans, or wishes. In my case, I would collect stamps on social work or hypnosis. Another example would be a plumber collecting stamps on plumbing. As you can imagine, topical collecting can enhance your life, expanding your motivation and opening doors. Many history teachers use postage stamps in their lesson plans.

Space exploration is another topic creating special excitement and limitless possibilities for growth. I remember when I requested Neil Armstrong's autograph on a first day cover in May of 1975. I received the following response later that month:

We are returning your first day cover unsigned.

> Professor Armstrong has been most generous in the past with his signature for these items. However, unfortunately for the sincere collector like your-self, this generosity has been somewhat abused by those requesting his signature on those items for commercial purposes.

> Since you are interested in obtaining his autograph, he has signed a photograph which we are happy to enclose.

> Sincerely,

> {signed)

> Secretary to
> Professor Neil A. Armstrong

At first, the letter response made me feel disappointed, but soon after, I was in awe, mesmerized, and thankful for his signed autograph (see figure 21).

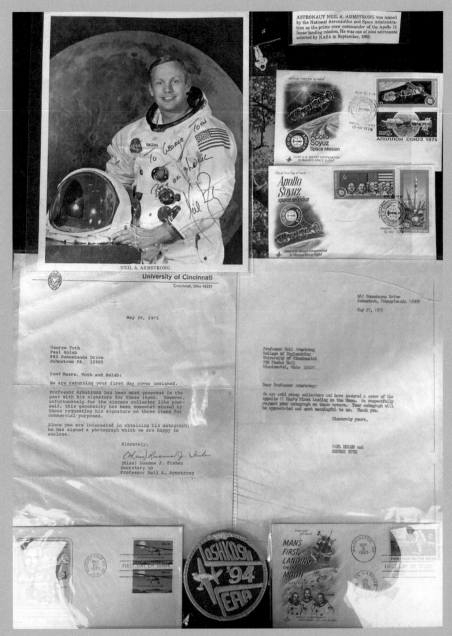

Figure 21: Autograph of Neil Armstrong and US Scott # 1569–1570 Apollo Soyuz Space Issue, 1975.

Another collecting example is stamps related to the military. This was of special interest to me because my birth year included the three stamps of the 1940 National Defense Issue: Scott #899–901 (see figure 22).

Figure 22: US Scott # 1899 to 901 National Defense. Issue First Day Cover, 1940.

Also, since I served in the army and worked with the Veterans Administration, US Military Academy, and Red Cross, many stamps hypnotized me as they crossed my work desk and in my spare time. A few of my favorites are US Scott #1016, #1004, #1013, and #3560 (see fgure 23).

Figure 23: US Scott # 1016 Red Cross Issue ,1952.
US Scott # 1004 Betsy Ross Issue, 1952.
US Scott # 1013 Service Woman Issue, 1952.
US Scott # 3560 US Army Military Academy Eagle and Shield, 2002.

Study stamps of your birth year, and experience how they might influence or expand your world. Topic interests can lead to amazing insights and exciting life adventures.

One of the best ways to use stamps as a conduit to healing is to conduct self-awareness exercises. The following exercise is the first of several presented throughout this book. These types of fun drills will help you think more clearly about yourself and your interests. They will help with your goals and overall wellness. You may be astonished by what you learn and feel.

Topic Exercise

Choose five topic areas that you may be aware of and interested in

- Topic 1:_____
- Topic 2:_____
- Topic 3:_____
- Topic 4:_____
- Topic 5:_____

Where might these areas lead you? If you need more space, use additional paper.

_____

_____

Many people have found healing uses for stamps in art, crafts, skills, and design. There are many imaginative possibilities for stress reduction and creativity. One example might be portraits of people and scenes comprised of stamps. These are made by combining colors and shapes from stamps, using them to form artistic images. A few are on display at the Franklin D. Roosevelt Museum in Hyde Park, New York. You could also use images of stamps on wallpaper, fabric, clothes, fashion designs, or ties. There are infinite creative possibilities to soothe the mind and body.

Puzzles and quizzes abound within the field of stamps. Many are officially documented in the Scott Catalogue. For example, look at figure 24, which includes both Scott #528 and #528b. Can you find the tiny dots that identify one stamp as Scott #528b, the 1920 two-cent Washington Type VII? If you look very closely, you will see the area above Washington's lip has four rows with three dots each. Due to World War I shortages, the Bureau of Engraving and Printing temporarily changed to offset printing to produce this stamp. The stamps paid the post-war first-class letter rate of two cents. Many were used, and then discarded. These stamps have an additional interesting factor. Do you know what it is? The stamp has an attached plate number. Each sheet of stamps has an identifying production number. It is rare and often highly collectable when left attached to the stamp.

Figure 24: US Scott # 528 George Washington, (with plate # 12142) 1920.
US Scott # 528b type Vll George Washington, (with plate # 12411), 1920.

I always thought fake stamps were made by unscrupulous people for the purpose of deceiving collectors. It was similar to making and passing fake twenty-dollar bills, which is a crime. Many fake stamps have emerged over the years. As stamps became more and more valuable, more and more imitation stamps emerged on the market. Fake stamps have become interesting and desirable, especially for people who cannot obtain, find, or afford originals. I'm not proposing that you do this. I'm just suggesting that you be aware of their existence. Most fake stamps are facsimiles of stamps that are extremely rare and expensive. They consist of varying quality. For example, I bought a fake Scott #294a Pan American with an inverted center for thirty dollars. As a real stamp, it's extremely rare and desirable because there are perhaps only one hundred known copies. It catalogs for $10,000. The fake stamp was made by taking a normal stamp and cutting out the center. The center is then placed upside down within the frame of the normal stamp, creating an inverted center. This is undetectable to the untrained eye. Why not develop a fantasy stamp hall of fame? Having fantasy stamps may provide a therapeutic way to satisfy your desire for rare unusual stamps and curb your unrealistic, over-expensive appetite (see figure 25).

Figure 25: US Scott # 294a Pan American Inverted Center FANTACY FACSIMILY
stamp (Center cut out variety L11). This is a forgery, clearly with center cut out and
reversed. It is considered a compelling looking stamp from the front, 1901.
Reverse image of Scott # 294a Pan American Inverted Center FANTACY Facsimile.

I have continuously been fascinated by the use of color in stamps. Color is universal. It's important in our history and in cultures around the world. Color has been ascribed to patterns of human behavior and personality traits. It often represents feelings. Here are some examples:

- red—passion, anger, and vibrancy
- orange—will power and sensuality
- yellow—cerebral and paternal
- green—vegetative and calmness
- blue—calmness, strength, and healing
- indigo—clairvoyance and far-sight
- violet—royalty and sorrow

Much has been studied about color on a conscious and subconscious level, including colors of the rainbow, the color wheel, and color's association with chakras. Color is important and has healing properties. Over the centuries and in various cultures, color associations may change. These connotations are often connected with personality traits or behaviors. For example, blue might mean calmness or strength.

I have listed twenty colors from the *Scott Specialized Catalog of United States Stamps and Covers*. I have also listed twenty colors from the 2021 *Burpee Seed Catalog* that can be found in nature. I was prompted by the color magenta. While looking through the seed catalog, I noticed a morning glory described as having magenta blooms. I immediately thought of the one-cent magenta stamp from British Guiana. Both sample lists of colors are equally fascinating and can be associated with healing properties in a similar, therapeutic way. It seems that many natural and man-made items have similar colors.

Colors of Scott Stamps	Colors of Flowers
magenta	magenta
apple	apple red velvet
azure	azure scarlet
bister	bister kentucky blue
blood	blood pastel orange
brilliant	brilliant vermillion red

burnt	burnt watermelon pink
cerise	cerise mandarin orange
chamois	chamois caramel yellow
cobalt	cobalt hungarian blue
crimson	crimson zinderella pink
heliotrope	heliotope tequila lime
genna	henna fuchsia
mauve	mauve orange pekoe
myrtle	myrtle deep burgundy
reseda	reseda lavender
salmon rose pink	pink
venetian	venetian blue moon
chocolate	chocolate
burning yellow	yellow

4

· ·

How Stamps May Affect Your Conscious and Subconscious Feelings

Hypnotic, amazing, superordinary, mesmerizing, unique, spectacular, and spellbinding are a few of the words that will come to mind as you explore the magic of postage stamps. They may touch your conscious and subconscious emotions. One of the world's most famous and celebrated postage errors in the United States is the tweny-four-cent airmail stamp issued in 1918, Scott #C4a (see figure 26).

Figure 26: US Scott # C3a Jenny Inverted Center and US Scott C3 Jenny , 1918.

It's referred to as the upside down "Jenny" airplane. A stamp collector named William Robey purchased a sheet of stamps at a Washington, DC, post office that had mistakenly printed the airplane upside down. The sheet of one hundred stamps was eventually numbered on the back side in 1970 and separated into singles and blocks, revealing the position of the stamps on the sheet. Over the years, the stamps have become more notable and famous, each developing its own provenance. The inverted "Jenny" stamps have a fascinating history of crime, romance, corruption, and greed. They have been sold, resold, lost, found, stolen, recovered, sued over, destroyed, and owned by some of history's most unusual people. Depending on their condition, these stamps have sold for as much as $1 million each. Much has been written about these stamps in George Amick's *The Inverted Jenny: Money, Mystery, and Mania*. It includes a brief history all ninety-six Jenny inverts accounted for in researched records.

The worlds' rarest stamp is the British Guiana (now Guyana) one-cent magenta. It was issued in limited numbers, and one specimen is known to exist in 1856. It is the only major stamp ever issued that is not represented in Britain's Royal Philatelic Collection. The stamp was originally found by a twelve-year-old boy in his uncle's collection. It was sold and went through numerous stamp collectors' hands until it was purchased by Irwin Weinberg. Weinberg was a stamp collector and dealer who represented a group of investors. In 1970, he bought the stamp at auction in New York City for $280,000—a record at the time. Although he purchased many rare stamps in the 1960s, including about eleven Scott #C4a Jennys, none brought as much attention as when he bought the one-cent magenta. In 1976, Weinberg went on to take the stamp to Philadelphia for the US Bicentennial. He also took the stamp to Japan, India, and Australia. He appeared on the television game show *To Tell the Truth* and Mike Douglas's talk show. He said that he wanted to "introduce the stamp to the world, and maybe find a buyer" (Barron 2016).

Weinberg had a flare for publicity and showmanship. On one occasion in 1978, while packing for a trip to Toronto with the stamp, he sent his son Jack to a military surplus store with instructions to buy a pair of handcuffs. On the plane, Weinberg quietly chained one of his own wrists to his briefcase. The handcuffs were a prop, a gimmick to get attention from news photographers who had been alerted to his arrival and the arrival of the world's most expensive stamp. The stamp was to be displayed at the Canadian Philatelic Exhibition. Weinberg went from the airport to a news conference for the exhibition. No one noticed that when he slipped the key into the handcuffs, it broke. He thought "just keep talking and worry about it later" (Barron 2016). Later, a firefighter provided a saw to cut off the handcuffs. This story of the stamp, handcuffs, and struggle to shed the shackles was picked up around the world.

In 1980, John DuPont, heir to the DuPont chemical fortune, paid $935,000 for the stamp at auction. He was convicted of third-degree murder in the 1996 shooting of Olympic wrestler David Schultz. Later du Pont was declared mentally ill. He died in prison in 2010. His estate sold the stamp for $9.5 million in 2014 (Barron 2017).

I remember receiving Irwin Weinberg's weekly newsletter, *Miner's Stamp News*, which listed his inventory of stamps for sale. One interesting point about publicity has stuck in my mind over the years. When I first received his newsletter in the mail, I couldn't help but notice that his return address stated that he was the "owner of the world's most valuable stamp" and included an image of the stamp (see figure 27).

Figure 27: British Guiana One Cent Black on Magenta 1856. The stamp last sold for 9.5 million dollars, making it the most valuable stamp in the world. Front and back side image has markings from previous owners.

After the stamp was sold, the return address was changed to the "former owner of the world's most valuable stamp." It was a genius example of creative advertising. He didn't have to actually own the stamp to use it for advertising. He could *not* own it and still continue to taut it. This struck me as amazing!

The Pan-American Exposition, held in Buffalo, New York, celebrated the advancements made during the nineteenth century. A series of six stamps honored engineering and industrial achievements. The issues were the first bicolored stamps produced by the Bureau of Engraving and Printing. They are prized by collectors. Three important errors were discovered in the bicolor printing process. Three different denominations had inverted centers caused by human error: Scott #294a #295a, and #296a. They were printed and sold.

I was fascinated and self-hypnotized by these errors to the point where I decided to purchase a one-cent Scott #294a at a New York City auction in the 1980s. I remember the day I traveled to the auction, bid on the stamp, and paid about $1,800 with my credit card. I convinced my father to travel with me to the Port Authority Building's parking lot by car, then take a taxi to the nearby auction gallery. Although my father thought I was crazy for spending that much money on a stamp, he was excited to accompany me and see what was happening at the auction. When we got to the auction building, we took an elevator to the auction floor with some well-dressed foreign travelers. We found our seats and waited for the auctioneer to announce Scott #294a. I kept bidding until the winning bid was mine. What excitement! I was hypnotized. I then paid for the stamp with my credit card and left for home without it. The standard arrangement was that the stamp would be mailed to me. It arrived several weeks later in a standard envelope with an unremarkable first-class stamp. I imagined more fanfare to match my excitement. When I finally got the stamp in my possession, all kinds of feelings surfaced in my state of mind, thoughts, and behaviors.

In 1999, I sold the stamp for about $5,000, using the money as part of the down payment for a home. Based on previous experience and knowledge, I can say that I'm a former owner of a Scott #294a—a commemorative 1901 one-cent, green and black Pan American with an inverted center—and a certificate of authenticity (see figure 28).

Figure 28: US 294a one cent Pan American Inverted Center, 1901 with certificate of authenticity by the Philatelic Foundation, dated 12/2/68.

Inverted centers hold a special excitement for me. They are very rare and expensive, especially when you think about how they were printed. Most are considered major errors and worth thousands of dollars depending on condition. Just looking at one actually hypnotizes me in many ways.

The error stamp has a dramatic appearance, showing a ship printed upside down by mistake. This is further emphasized since it is one of the first commemorative US stamps printed in two colors: green and black. Some of these stamps were purchased and used as one-cent postage. The postally used stamps are actually scarcer than the mint stamps since there are less of them. The used stamps made it through the postal system; they were postmarked and discovered at a later time.

An inversion error can occur with bicolor stamps because the stamp must pass through the printing machine once for each color. If the second color is inserted into the printing apparatus the wrong way or backward, the second image will appear upside down on each stamp on the sheet. Apparently, these errors are often difficult to detect. I believe the used copies were undetected. The ship was probably placed on the envelope right side up and sent through the postal system. When attached to the envelope this way, the frame of the stamp appears upside down. This might go undetected by the average user. Can you imagine finding one of these inverts? How would you feel? How would you safeguard it? Where would you keep it? Would you tell others about it?

Actual ownership of this stamp had various hypnotic effects on me. I seemed to start having different feelings that were generally unexplained at the time. I was proud to own the stamp. I felt senses of accomplishment and achievement. I also had an increased sense of responsibility because I had the concern to insure the stamp against theft, damage, or loss. I even wanted to safeguard the stamp in other ways, such as renting a safe-deposit box at a bank. With this purchase, I had increased my financial investment, security, stability, and diversity. I had a greater feeling of self-worth gained by owning of a rare, global, desirable, historic, and well-documented collectible. I felt like I was an above average collector—a collector of *rare* stamps. Now I had a secret. But what would happen if I shared it? How would it affect me, my family, and my friends? I was also concerned with selling the stamp. How would I feel placing it back in a stamp auction? Should I sell it outright to a dealer or collector or trade it for something else?

I was inspired by Scott #294a and became interested in other inversion errors. Some of these stamps were less expensive, but they were just as intriguing. Three examples come to mind. The first is Canal Zone Scott #39e (see figure 29).

Figure 29: Canal Zone Scott 39e Two cent Inverted Center MAJOR ERROR 1912–1916.

This two-cent stamp with an inverted center was a major error made from 1912 to 1916. Another such stamp was US Internal Revenue Scott #R135b (see figure 30).

Figure 30: US Internal Revenue Scott R135b INVERTED
CENTER George Washington, 1871.

This stamp featured an inverted George Washington at its center. The final example is US Internal Revenue Scott #R115a (see figure 31).

Figure 31: US internal Revenue Scott # R115a George Washington INVERTED CENTER with a few wayward perforations 1871.

This stamp had two errors: an inverted center and a few wayward perforations. How do these inverted centers make you feel?

The hypnotic effects of inverted centers led me to believe that I liked certain stamps because of the way they made me feel. I can feel different intensity levels for each stamp. These emotional states mainly depend on what the stamp commermorates, represents, or suggests in my conscious and subconscious mind as well as the date of issue. The reasons for these feelings and mindsets may be infinate and far reaching, validating my belief that postage stamps are outstanding tools for therapy and healing.

The Graf Zeppelin was the most successful rigid airship ever. Between 1928 and 1937, it flew more than a million miles. Three stamps were issued to commemorate the Zeppelin's first round-trip voyage from Europe to North and South America—Scott #13, #14, and #15 (see figure 32).

Figure 32: US Scott # C13-15 Graf Zeppelin Issue. 1930.

Although 3.26 million Zeppelin stamps were printed, 90 percent were destroyed, making them very desirable and expensive. Many collectors dream about owning one. The Zeppelin stamps enthrall me every time I see them.

With the start of home mail delivery in 1862, a two-cent stamp was needed. Scott #73 picturing Andrew Jackson was issued. Interestingly, CSA Scott #8, an 1873 Confederate two-cent stamp, uses the same Miner Kilbourne Kellog portrait miniaturized by John Wood Dodge. Therefore, the United States of America and the Confederate States of America had two-cent stamps with the same Jackson portrait during the Civil War (see figure 33).

Figure 33: US Scott 73 Andrew Jackson (Blackjack) 1861
Confederate States General Issue Scott # 8 Andrew Jackson, 1863.

A series of sixteen commemorative stamps called the Columbians was issued in 1893. These stamps are among the most beautifully engraved and sought-after stamps around the world. They were issued to commemorate the Columbian Exposition, which celebrated the one hundreth anniversary of Christopher Columbus's discovery of the New World. Each attractively engraved stamp tells a portion of the exploration. Only a fraction of collectors will ever own a complete set because less than 25,000 of the four- and five-dollar stamps made it into the hands of collectors. Those two values now sell for over $2,000 each. On the other hand, Scott #231, with a two-cent value, sells for twenty cents. Scott #231c has a defect called the "Broken Hat Variety." During the printing process, a break occurred in the printing press transfer roll. If you check the hat on the man to the left of Columbus, you can see a nick. Some nicks are wider than others because the break in the plate widened gradually. Scott #231c sells for sixty-five dollars (see figure 34).

Figure 34: US Scott 231c Columbian Exposition "BROKEN HAT VARIETY."
Close up image shows break in plate creating broken hat variety.

Many people consider Scott #292 to be the most beautiful US stamp (see figure 35).

Figure 35: US Scott # 292 Trans–Mississippi Exposition "Western Cattle in Storm," 1898.

It was based on a famous Scottish painting called *The Vanguard*. Painted in 1878 by John A. MacWhirter, *The Vanguard* shows cattle in a winter storm in Scotland. Many collectors consider this one of the finest US stamps ever produced. It incorrectly specified that the image was of cattle in the western United States. The canvas image was also copied without permission from Lord Blyswood, the owner. A full apology was given.

Back-of-the-book stamps are often little known and obscure. *Back of the book* generally refers to special stamps used for purposes other than postage. They are usually placed at the end of stamp albums or catalogs. Examples include postage dues, revenues, postal savings, semiofficial, and registration stamps. They seem to be more popular as collectibles today than years ago. I consider them intriguing and very desirable. Hawaii began issuing these stamps when the Stamp Duty Act was passed in 1876. The first eight designs were printed by the American Bank Note Company and had detailed engravings. These stamps were in use for over thirty years. The purpose of these stamps was not for letter or package postage. Revenue stamps covered new taxes on deeds, agreements, and other documents. The early issues were all rouletted. From 1886 until it was outlawed in 1888, HR Scott #3 was used to pay the tax on opium. From 1898 to 1900, the tax on stock certificates was twenty cents, but the supply of twenty-cent stamps was almost depleted. To solve this problem, the government decided to overprint HR Scott #1, valuing it down to twenty cents from twenty-five cents (see figure 36).

Figure 36: Hawaii HR Scott # 1 Tax on Stock Certificate from 25 cents to 20 cents. Hawaii HR Scott # 7 20 cent Green Rouletted Revenue Stamp.

According to the Scott Catalogue, postal-savings stamps are considered part of a special philatelic category of stamps. This category includes slightly different kinds of stamps issued at different times by the post office or US Treasury Department. The stamps highlighted here were issued in 1941. They came in ten-cent to five-dollar denominations and served as a means for ordinary citizens to save or invest a little bit at a time. The investments were loans to the federal government. PS Scott #11 and #15 were given to me by my mother when I was a teen collector. Of course, I continue to be hypnotized by the five-dollar and ten-cent stamps. The ten-cent stamp is in the form of a handmade pin or broach to support the efforts in World War II (see figure 37).

Figure 37: US Postal Savings Scott # 11 and Scott # 15.

The ten cent stamps are in the form of a pin or brooch to show support efforts in World War II, 1941.

The US revenue stamp of 1879 was used to show that newspaper and periodical taxes were prepaid. These scarce stamps were only sold to publishers, making them difficult to find. The helmet of Mercury special delivery stamp is considered one of the most artistic US stamps ever produced. It was on sale at post offices for only six months. When it was issued, the design was highly criticized. Critics called it the "Merry Widow" after a popular play of the era (see figure 38).

Figure 38: US Scott # SD 5 E7 Special Delivery Helmut of Mercury , 1908.

The Wells Fargo western express cover offers the owner a direct link to the California gold rush, the pony express, and the American Indian Wars. This cover shows the special Wells Fargo woodcut frank. The woodcut mark acted as a postage stamp, showing that the fee was prepaid. Historic penmanship, backstamps, and various routing marks tell of each cover's history—often dangerous journeys, dusty mining towns, and stagecoach trips through American Indian territories. This offers a unique historical window into the past! The gold-rush era was 1849, and it created a need for western express companies. (see figure 39).

Figure 39: US Local Stamps and Carriers Scott # 143L3 Blue San Francisco Running Pony cancellation Position R9 – BROKEN LEG PRINTING FLAW (Front Hoof Missing), very rare – only 10 examples known to exist, 1861.

Wells Fargo became the largest and most successful one. In 1852, American Express refused to open offices in California. Henry Wells and William Fargo, both directors at American Express, opened their own company in California. They bought gold, sold paper bank drafts, and delivered valuables—including mail. They used pony express riders, stage coaches, steamboats, and railroads to deliver goods. Wells Fargo and dozens of other private express companies were important to life in early western development. In order to operate and guarantee payment, Wells Fargo bought thousands of three-cent stamped envelopes from the US post office and printed "Wells Fargo" on them. This was how mail was carried at a premium price. The post office had a legal monopoly on first-class mail. In the early 1890s, they forced Wells Fargo to stop carrying the mail (see figure 40).

Figure 40: US Wells Fargo Cover Three cent Wells Fargo and Company
Cover to San Francisco with blue February 9 cancel, 1871.

Figure shows Scott #143L3 with a very rare and famous defect. It features a broken-leg printing flaw. Only ten examples are known to exist.

Jaime Escalante (1930–2010) was a high school calculus teacher. He demonstrated that with hard work and determination, supposedly unteachable students could learn even the most difficult subjects. Born in Bolivia, he became a teacher in the United States. He offered to teach calculus classes so that his students would be allowed to take college-level courses, preparing them to take the advanced placement calculus exam. When fourteen of his students passed the notoriously difficult exam in 1982, they were accused of cheating. Escalante suspected the reason was because they were Mexican Americans from a low-income area of Los Angeles. Twelve students took a second version of the same exam, and they all passed. Escalante and his students attracted national attention with the release of the 1988 movie *Stand and Deliver*. Escalante became one of the most famous teachers in America, and in 1989, he was inducted into the National Teachers Hall of Fame. He believed that a teacher's role was to encourage students to set high goals and achieve beyond their expectations. His legacy lives on in all teachers who see potential in each of their students. In 2016, US Scott # 5100 was issued in his honor (see figure 41).

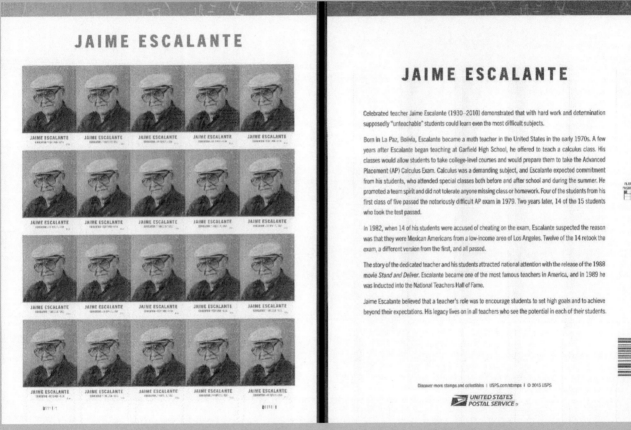

Figure 41: US Scott # 5100 Jamie Escalante, High School Calculus Teacher Forever Sheet of 20 stamps.

5

· ·

How to Apply Hypnosis and Self-Hypnosis to Gain Insight and Improvement

I'm not aware of any psychotherapists or clinical hypnotists combining stamps and hypnotism together to be used as a powerful growth force in behavioral health treatment. Stamps provide power and incentives to learn and grow in unparalleled ways. This happens to individuals on the conscious level. If you add the concept of psychotherapy and hypnotism, you begin to provide powerful incentives for learning and growing in unparalleled ways on the subconscious level. This may often add another dimension to a person's life. It can begin to affect the way you think, feel, and behave. It can act as a gyroscope to your personality, affecting your balance of life in all areas—physically, mentally, and spiritually. In order to see this more clearly, I will briefly explain what hypnotism is and how it works. All of this can be summed up with one statement: stamps combined with hypnosis equal an improved balance of health and life.

Hypnotism or hypnosis can be defined in many ways. Hypnosis is simply shifting back and forth between the conscious and subconscious mind—a natural process that occurs about 90 percent of every day. The conscious mind only uses about 10 percent of our brain. It analyzes, thinks, and plans and houses our short-term memories. The subconscious mind stores our long-term memories and aids with our developmental stages. It also controls our emotions and feelings, habitual patterns, relationship patterns, addictions, involuntary bodily functions, creativity, intuition, and spiritual connections.

We naturally and automatically shift between conscious and subconscious. How many times have you been driving along the highway and missed your exit? You were probably under the subconscious level in hypnosis. While driving, you were fully alert and in control of yourself at all times. There are many myths about hypnosis. Myths are false beliefs that often place the truth in doubt. It's important to clear up these false beliefs. While hypnotized, you cannot be controlled or made to do something that you don't want to do. You are in total control of yourself at all times and fully aware of your surroundings. You are completely awake. No one can make you walk or quack like a duck.

When under hypnosis, you are in a state of relaxation. Your mind is clear, tranquil, and more open to suggestions. This highly suggestible state of mind is more receptive to emotions, feelings, and long-term memories. This level may be reached by a hypnotist counting down to level one. Level one is the bottom of relaxation, and level ten is the higest state of awareness. When at level one, the hypnotist may make positive suggestions about new and desired changes of behaviors, ways of thinking, and feelings. These are often called short-term or long-term imprints. With some practice, you can reach this level of relaxation by yourself through a process called self-hypnosis. You can develop your own ways to relax and meditate, achieving similar goals.

In order to spread the idea that stamps can improve your life, I developed a two-hour course and presented it as an adult education class at the Desmond campus in Newburgh, New York. Ten students attended. The class was a huge success. The students seemed astonished at the influence postage stamps had and how they could be connected to personal feelings, education, and positive growth. The presentation was powerful. It served as a background model for some of the ideas and motivation for this book. For this reason, I have developed the course outline and presentation write-up as follows:

Course title: "How to Liven Up Your Life with Postage Stamps: Improve the Way You Think, Feel, and Behave

Course length: Two hours

Goals of course: You will be able to:

- think globally and learn about world events;
- expand your knowledge of the nature of people;

- increase your awareness of the world;
- feel better, happier, more relaxed, and less stressed;
- learn about art, color, and shapes and what they evoke;
- behave more positively;
- increase motivation and energy; and
- create new ideas.

Course description: This course unearths magic pathways to personal development and the expansion of knowledge of world events. Develop a personal toolbox of relaxation and stress-reduction techniques. Expand your interests, think more clearly, increase concentration, be more confident, and improve your mindfulness. This may be the most significant course you have ever taken.

I showed the class ten slides of stamps in a PowerPoint presentation. Those stamp slides are also revealed in this book. A video or recording of this class is not available online, but all of the relevant material can be found in this book. It is therefore not nescessary to view the course to effectively use the book.

One student was very excited and amazed after seeing an image of the one-cent magenta stamp from British Guiana. The student indicated that she had been born in British Giana and never new about the stamp before this class. Another student became very thrilled and emotional after seeing an image of Scott #1530 from the Universal Postal Union issue (see figure 42).

Figure 42: US Scott # 1530 Universal Postal Issue – Raphael First Day Cover. 1974.
Vatican Rome Painting.
What part of this Italy, Vatican Painting shows the image of the stamp?

This ten-cent stamp showed Michelangelo in Raphael's *School of Athens*. Inscribed on the stamp was "letters mingle souls" from a letter by poet John Donne. In the class discussion, the student explained that she had met her husband in Italy and had the inscription on her wedding ring. These were unforgettable, hypnotic moments that will enhance those two lives forever.

6

Inspiring Examples of
Private Practice Cases

How does one bridge the gap between just having an interest in postage stamps and using them as a healing conduit for treatment of behavioral health. Is that a big gap? Not really. If you study the history of mental health treatments, you will find that they go back hundreds of years. The history of postage stamps, however, began in 1847. As behavioral health treatments continue to change and evolve, new methods and approaches are uncovered. This often occurs when previous methods don't work or when unusual and emergency circumstances arise, sometimes when you least expect them.

I have found that most people seek behavioral health treatment because they are very motivated and intelligent enough to want to change or improve the ways they think, feel, and behave. Many want to feel better about themselves and be more confident, productive, and optimistic. They want to be happier in every way. I strongly believe that involvement with postage stamps provides a special pathway to achieving these goals and much, much more. A domino effect often occurs, causing other benefits to take place. Do not underestimate the power of stamps. Use your native intelligence, and take a chance. Stamps will have a profound, positive effect, connecting your mind, body, and spirit. The following are actual case examples on the use of postage stamps as conduits to change, improvement, and healing from my private psychotherapy practice.

Case 1

John was a married forty-five-year-old male. He lived with his wife and two children (ages fifteen and twelve). John was often depressed and had frequent anxiety attacks that prevented him from working as an office manager. I gave him the therapeutic task of listing the US stamps that were issued in his birth year of 1975. At his next session, I placed him under hypnosis and asked him to select a stamp from the list that appealed to him. He chose the ten-cent Scott #1558 (see figure 43).

Issue Date: March 13, 1975
First Day City: Washington, D.C.
Designer: Robert Hallock
          Newton, Connecticut
Modeler: Peter Cocci
Press: Andreotti gravure
Colors: Light blue, orange, dark
          blue, and purple
Image Area: 1.44 x 0.84 inches or
          36.576 x 21.336 millimeters
Plate Numbers: Four
Stamps to Pane: 50
Selvage: "Mail Early in the Day"
          "Use ZIP Code" and "Mr. ZIP"

Collective Bargaining Commemorative Stamp

The third U. S. commemorative stamp of 1975 salutes Collective Bargaining, a social force that stabilized labor-management relations in the United States.

Collective Bargaining originated in the nineteenth century. But it was then a minor part of a civil rights movement. Labor's main goal at the time was to correct the injustices of the industrial revolution. It was not, as now, to negotiate fixed-term contracts on wages and other terms and conditions of employment.

Modern Collective Bargaining began in 1935 when Congress imposed on employers in the Wagner Act the duty to bargain collectively with the majority representative of their employees. Twelve years later, in Taft-Hartley, Congress imposed a similar duty on unions. Both unions and employers were now required to bargain collectively, to negotiate in good faith and to reduce their agreements to writing.

Among other stamps, Robert Hallock also designed the Veterans of Foreign Wars commemorative of 1974 and the Stone Mountain issue of 1970.

Requests for first day cancellations should contain the proper remittance and should be addressed to "Collective Bargaining Stamp, Postmaster, Washington, DC 20013." Orders must be postmarked by March 13.

USPS Stamp Poster 75-3

Figure 43: US Scott # 1558 Souvenir Page SP # 362 Collective Bargaining 100s/s First Day Cover, 1975.

During the session, he felt the power and support that the stamp represented for first-line working employees. The more he learned about what the stamp represented, the better he felt. The following session, he indicated that his anxiety attacks were reduced. He was able to return to work and feel better. He was intrigued by the stamp and what it signified. Information about the collective bargaining laws gave him the knowledge and confidence to begin resolving some of his issues at work.

Case 2

Mary Ellen was a twenty-five-year-old female who lived alone. She had just lost her job as a child day care provider because of changes to internal funding requirements. She became depressed and was not happy about work opportunities or the cost of living in New York. I asked her to list the US stamps issued in her birth year of 1995. She was placed under hypnosis during the next session and immediately chose Scott #2050 (see figure 44).

FLORIDA STATEHOOD
150th Anniversary

Florida will celebrate its sesquicentennial of statehood in 1995. The 27th American state, it was admitted to the Union March 3, 1845.

Three centuries ago, in 1513, Juan Ponce de Leon discovered Florida, named it and claimed it for Spain. France and England also tried to establish permanent settlements in the region, but all three countries ultimately failed. In 1819, Spain agreed to transfer Florida to the United States. Future President Andrew Jackson served briefly as provisional governor before the Territory of Florida was organized in 1822.

Costly wars with native Seminole Indians slowed Florida's progress during the 1830s. Nevertheless, as the decade drew to a close, residents drafted a constitution in preparation for statehood. They were forced to wait six years because Congress was determined to maintain the balance between free states and slave states, of which Florida was one. When their petition was finally approved, Democrat William D. Moseley became the first state governor. He presided over a government estab-

lished in the capital city of Tallahassee. Florida's development was interrupted again in the 1860s, this time by the Civil War. When the war was over, however, Florida experienced a period of enormous expansion. Swampland was drained and opened for development, citrus groves were planted, and resort cities sprang up along the coast. By the year 1900, the state's population had grown to more than 525,000.

Since World War I, Florida has been one of the fastest-growing states in the nation, and now ranks fourth in population. The local economy is partially fueled by a huge agricultural output of fruits, vegetables, and nuts. Even more important is the tourist industry, which accounts for annual revenues of nearly $32 billion. One of the state's leading attractions is Everglades National Park, a vast subtropical wilderness with large populations of crocodiles, alligators, turtles, and swamp birds.

The 32¢ U.S. stamp marking Florida's 150th year of statehood was designed by Laura Smith of Hollywood, California.

Figure 44 US Scott # 2950 Anniversary of Florida Statehood
FIRST DAY COVER, including Florida State history.

This thirty-two-cent stamp celebrated Florida's 150th anniversary of statehood. She liked the stamp since she was born in Florida. She reevaluated her living circumstances and decided to move back. Jobs were more readily available in Florida, and the economy was less expensive.

Case 3

Joe was a single forty-seven-year-old male. He was seeking a way to gain more confidence in his life. He saw many therapists over the years but wasn't able to find a way to achieve his goal. After several sessions, I asked him if he had a hero. This hero could be alive or deceased, fictional or real. Joe explained that George Washington was his hero. He was a Revolutionary War hero and the first president of the United States. I could tell that Joe strongly admired this historic, legendary figure. I placed him into a state of hypnosis and gave him Scott #4504 as a gift (see figure 45).

Figure 45: US Scott # 4504 Twenty Cent Georg 1977e Washington Full Sheet of twenty stamps.

The stamp was in a protective mount. I directed Joe to place it safely in his pocket or wallet so that he could carry it at all times. Depicting his hero, the stamp would give Joe the confidence and power to do the things he wanted. It worked.

With clients, I often call on a hero to assist with the support they need. Postage stamps are loaded with hero images, both fictitious and real. I usually keep several common hero stamps in my office that are available for "use" whenever called upon. They do the job every time. My most common heroes are George Washington, Superman, and Superwoman. Others include President John F. Kennedy, Douglas MacArthur, Babe Ruth, Mother Teresa, Ty Cobb, Dorothea Dix, Eleanor Roosevelt, Sojourner Truth, Duke Kahanamoku, Wonder Woman, Green Lantern, and Batman.

Case 4

Jose was a fifteen-year-old male high schooler who wanted to try hypnosis to improve his soccer abilities. He was able to locate a commemorative postage stamp related to soccer, and it was with him during the hypnosis session. He was placed under hypnosis with the following script:

> For any person who has ever played soccer, whether professionally or amateurishly, there seems to be days when we felt we were going to lose for sure. It is amazing how on those days when we woke up and felt like we were gong to win, we had the ability to do just that. We did win. However, on those days when we woke up and felt like we would probably lose, we usually did. From this moment on, before you start to play soccer, you are going to have a winning feeling. You are going to feel confident that you will win and be the best that you can ever, ever be. If the thought of losing comes to your mind, you will be able to shut it down. You will turn it off and think the way a winner thinks. As you practice thinking like a winner, you become a winner. With every day that passes, your talents and motivation become greater and greater. You are becoming the best that you can ever, ever be. (Mottin 2005, 128)

Jose was a winner and a collector of sports stamps after just one session. His collection includes Laos Scott #109 of the Mexican Soccer World Cup and Laos Scott #684, which depicts a soccer souvenir sheet (see figure 46).

Figure 46: Laos Scott # 109 Mexico Soccer World Cup, 1986.
Laos Scott # 684 Soccer Souvenir Sheet Mexico World Cup, 1985.

Case 5

Judy was a thirty-five-year-old female student who had a fear of flying and was willing to try hypnosis to do away with it. I introduced the idea of finding a postage stamp with an airplane image to support the hypnotic process. I located Scott #C32 (see figure 47).

Figure 47: US Scott # C32 Sky Master Airplane block of four
SMARTCRAFT typed First Day Cover, 1946,

Placing her under hypnosis, I said, " Now with your eyes closed, I want you to think of the bravest person in the whole world. It might be someone real. It might be someone imaginary. As you begin to know who the bravest person in the whole world is, I want you to shake your head yes. Good. I want you to tell me who that person is."

"It's Amelia Earhart," Judy replied.

"Amelia Earhart was pretty brave. Amelia Earhart probably wasn't afraid of anything was she? No, and if you were Amelia Earhart's friend—if she could be with you—you would not be afraid either, would you? No."

Sierra Leone Scott #200103b depicts the eighty-fifth anniversary of Amelia Earhart's solo flight (see figure 48).

Figure 48: Sierra Leone Scott # 200103b Aviator Amelia Earhart to stamp sheet commemorating the 85th Anniversary of solo flight from Hawaii to California, 2020.

7

· ·

Visual Imagery Exercises to Reduce Stress and Anxiety

Visual imagery is a hypnotic technique that promotes relaxation, problem-solving, creativity, and personal well-being. It is a powerful and natural tool that can be used to help encourage change. It supports the concept that the mind and body work together and influence each other. The mental can affect the physical, and the physical can affect the mental. This concept is not new. It has been known for years. However if we add postage stamps, the dynamics and benefits can be enhanced. Imagine finding stamps from various countries in the world related to healing, enhancing self-esteem, relaxation, problem-solving, spiritual centering, peak performance, or stress management.

Select a stamp from a catalog, album, or online computer device, and place it in front of you. Use the stamp as a base or center point for your visual imagery. Scripts can be used in several ways. Someone can read or present a script to you as you follow along with your imagination. Or you can just imagine the script yourself, either reading or thinking about it. You can also just "daydream" the story in the script. It may help to be in a comfortable, quiet room. You may add soft music. Do whatever helps you feel more comfortable and whatever works. I have included some examples of visual imageries that you may use.

US Scott #1610

Figure 49 (use for stress management and relaxation).

Figure 49: US Scott # 1610 Rush Lamp and Candle Holder 1979.
US Scott # 1610 First Day Cover

It's time to daydreaming. Time to relax in peace and quiet … …

Time to clear your mind of clutter… …and focus on the images that calm and sooth you … …

As you begin to slow down and relax, gently close your eyes …

Turn your attention inward… …Notice your breathing and the surfaces that support you … …

Notice the images that cross your mind… … as you clear your mental landscape … … …

As you continue to relax deeper and deeper … …

Imagine yourself in a dark quiet room … … …

A candle is set on a table in the corner of the room … … … The candle may be similar to the candle image of the Rush Lamp in front of you (or any other stamp selected by the individual that represents a candle).

Imagine yourself striking a match, lighting the candle, and blowing out the match … … … … … … … … … … … … Pause for a few seconds … … … … … …

Focus your attention on the candle … …

As the initial smoke from the wick flickers up into the air … … … …

The blue flame creeps slowly downward, towards the melting wax … … … …

Creating a small pool of liquid on the top of the candlestick … … … …

As the wick burns, this pool slowly becomes too large for the space holding it … and it starts to overflow … much like the tension stored in your body … that builds up and seeks release

… … … … … … … … … … … … … … … Pause for a few seconds … … … … … … … … … … … …

As you continue to watch your candle, the first drop of melted wax …

Escapes the lip of the pool … … and slides down the side … … … …

Then another drop slides down, … … … and another … … …

Followed by a slow steady stream of melted wax

Melting, … … … … … … … oozing … … … … escaping … … … dripping … … … sliding … … …

… … … … … … … … … … … … … … … Pause for a few seconds … … … … … … … … … …

Now imagine that the melting wax ... ... is the tension in your mind and body ... ...

Melting ... ...oozing ... ... escaping ... ... dripping ... ... sliding ... ...
Finding its own release ... ...

... ... Longer pause ... ...

When you are ready ... ... Blow out the candle and return your focus to the present moment ... ...

And to your surroundings ... ...

Now open your eyes ... ... bringing back with you a sense of release and calm from the melting candle. (Schwartz 1995, 46–47)

Iceland Scott #438

Figure 50 (use for healing and problem solving).

Figure 50: South Africa – Venda Scott # SG 42–SG45 Lakes and Waterfalls, 1981.
The stamps on the FIRST DAY COVER were selected to represent self- healing and problem solving.

It's daydreaming time. Time to relax in peace and quiet.

Take a deep breath and gently close your eyes ... ...

Let your eyes relax and be comfortable ... ...

Your eyes are relaxed and your lids are heavy ... ...

And any tension you might be carrying in your forehead is just melting away ... ...

You are floating gently and softly into a wonderful state of relaxation ... ...

As you continue to relax ... ...

Imagine that you are hiking in a remote wooded area, perhaps much like the area pictured in the Iceland stamp! (or any stamp of your choosing) ... ... and far from any roads, towns, or people ... ...

... ... Pause about 10 seconds ... ...

You come across a crystal clear stream of water ... ...

It appears that no one has ever been in this part of the woods before ... ... and the stream is completely pure and natural ... ...

You are in a state of awe ... ...

Thirsty from your hiking ... ...

You kneel down along the mossy shoreline to drink ... ...

Taste how crisp and fresh this water is ... ...

Feel this water entering into your body ... ...

As it is absorbed within you ... ...

Every cell in your body is revitalized from your head to the tips of your toes ... ...

... ... Pause for several seconds ... ...

This sensation is an experience to be shared ... ...

Bring it back with you as you open your eyes and return from your hiking journey

You are relaxed and revitalized in every way. (Schwartz 1995, 203-204)

In this particular exercie, you may direct the healing water to an area in the body where the client wants relief from pain. Adapt the script to meet the client's needs.

Scott #956
See Figure 51 (use for spiritual centering and self-esteem).

Figure 51: US Scott # 956 Four Chaplains Issue Flugel multi-color cachet and single stamp.

Relax and focus on your breathing ... ...

As your eyes gently close, let your mind wander and drift now to buoyancy ... ... floating ... ... drifting ... ... and relaxing ... ...

Just relax and listen to the words I speak ... allow yourself to relax, relax, and relax ... ... (listen or imagine the list of words)

Comfort ... ... release ... ... coast ... ... ease ... open ... mellow out ... ... loose ... tranquil ... ... refresh ... ... bask ... loose ... ... tranquil ... ... refresh ... ... bask ... slacken ... free ... revitalize ... enjoy ... ... delight ... ... diminish ... ... peaceful ... ... savor ... loaf ... ... taper off ... free thoughts ... siesta ... ... rest ... lessen ... energize ... ... soften ... unwind ... ... unbend ... ... carefree ... ... pause ... at ease ... ... breathe easy ... float ... wane ... ... recline ... ... serene ... ... repose ... ... lie down ... ... feathery ... ... take your time ... ... relief ... ... and relax ... ...

Now imagine at this moment
That you are sitting on the shore of a protected lake ...
It is very peaceful and calm and the water is a deep, deep blue ...
The lake is surrounded by trees ... ...
The trees have full, green leaves hanging from their branches ...
Imagine a single drop of dew resting on a leaf ... water
The leaf is on a tree which hangs over an expanse of flat undisturbed water ... ...
As the dew rolls down the leaf ...
Feel tension giving way to gravity ...
Gradually releasing hold of the leaf ... ...
Then falling slowly toward the water ... ...
As the dewdrop is welcomed into the water, imagine the ripples it creates ...
Each enlarges slowly and gradually ...
This continues as its action is absorbed by the lake ...
Soon the lake is back to a relaxed, undisturbed, and smooth state once again.
It is no longer a single falling drop ... ...
You are now part of a large breadth of calm, soothing water.
In your calm and soothing state of mind, you may now tune back into here and now ...
It is time to awaken. (Schwartz 1995, 201–202)

Scott #1387
Figure 52 (use to enhance relaxation and creativity).

Figure 52: US Scott 1387, American Bald Eagle, NATURAL HISTORY ISSUE. US Scott 1837-1390 FIRST DAY COVER PLATE BLOCK, 1970.

As you relax and listen to my voice ... (allow pauses as needed)

Think of yourself melting into the most comfortable chair you own ... ...

As your body releases and becomes very relaxed ... ...

Allow the feeling of weightlessness to take over ... ...

Gently close your eyes ...

And feel yourself floating ... ... weightless and free ...

Imagine yourself resting outside ... under a clear blue sky ... ...

And as you look up ... ... you see a magnificent bald eagle ...

Seemingly motionless and buoyant ...

The eagle floats along the gentle currents of the wind ... ...

Moving effortlessly forward ...

As it moves ...

You move in harmony with the bird ... ...

Towards a state of serene relaxation ... ...

Imagine yourself rising ... ...

And soaring away from your tension and frustration ... ...

And motionless and buoyant on your own currents of relaxation ... ...

As the eagle slowly glides and drifts toward the horizon ... ...

Become more and more aware of your body and your room ... ...

And gently open your eyes and awaken. (Schwartz 1995, 90–91)

Scott #2208

Figure 53 (use for peak performance and to cope under stress).

Figure 53: US Scott # 2208 Blue Fish Tuna single stamp
US Scott # 2208 Blue fish Tuna , and Gold FIRST DAY COVER, WITH
22kt GOLD REPLICA Postal Commemorative Society, 1986.

Sand, water and warm weather ...

A favorite setting to imagine resting ... ... relaxing ... ...

And closing your eyes ... ...

Take time to imagine resting and relaxing right now ... ...

As you gently close your eyes ... ...

Imagine that you are at the beach in a place of tropical beauty ... ...

Pause

You are standing on a sandy beach ... ...

You breathe in deeply ... ...

And exhale fully ...

It is warm OR It's warm, and as you approach the water ... ...

You see that it is calm clear, and shallow ... ...

You spot a small, colorful tropical fish in shallow water ...

Coming to the shore ... ... to rest where it is less turbulent ... ...

Choosing a safe spot, this vibrant fish remains buoyant ... ... watch the fins moving gently in the water ... ...

Keeping the fish at the same depth ... ...

The fish appears unconscious of its efforts to remain buoyant ... ...

Pause

Let this buoyancy linger in your mind ... ... until you feel as though you are light and floating yourself ... ...

Pause

Feeling light and buoyant ... ...

Allow this sensation to carry you back here ... ...

To the present and to the room ... ... and now awaken and open your eyes. (Schwartz 1995, 173–174)

Wonderful Stamp

Select your own stamp that makes you feel better, stronger, more confident, and a greater sense of balance. For example, you may use one of the stamps in figures 54, 55, 56, 57, or 58.

Figure 54: Caribbean Nevis Art Stamps, Leonardo Da Vinci, Mona Lisa Painting 1 value, imperforate Souvenir Sheet, 2019.

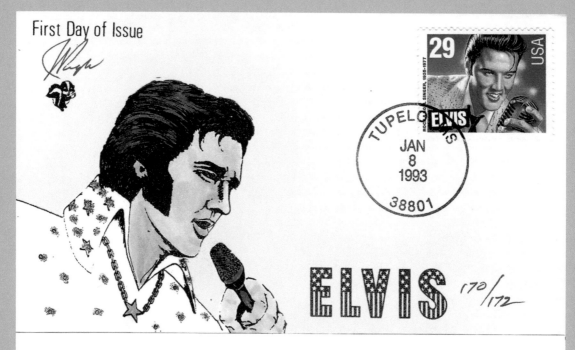

First Day of Issue

29 USA

ROCK 'N' ROLL SINGER, 1935-1977

TUPELO MS
JAN
8
1993
38801

ELVIS

ELVIS 170/172

Julian & Sharon Pugh
PUGH CACHETS, INC.
(713) 363-9135

P O Box 8789
The Woodlands, TX
77387-8789

Elvis Aaron Presley - The Vegas Years - Item 93-004

Elvis Aaron Presley was one of twin boys born to Gladys Smith Presley and Vernon Elvis Presley on January 8, 1935 in Tupelo, MS. His brother, Jesse Garon Presley, died within six hours of their birth. Early life in Tupelo was rather typical of poor middle class folk of the period and Elvis' upbringing in the South gave him a deep seated belief in God, respect for his elders, and a patriotic love for his country.

His success as a musical recording artist was meteoric for he went from a truck driver making a salary of $41 a week to a star with seventeen successive million selling singles in less than three years. His first musical hit was "Heartbreak Hotel" (1955) and during the next five years, nearly every song he recorded ranked among America's Top 10. "Heartbreak Hotel" became the first record in history to reach Number One on the Billboard Country and Western, Rhythm and Blues and Pop charts all in the same week. He won three Grammy's and all were for recordings of religious songs.

Figure 55: US Scott # 2721 Elvis stamp on PUGH designed/painted Elvis "The Vegas Years" FIRST DAY COVER (170 OF 172), 1993.

Figure 56: US Scott # 4084 DC Comics Superheroes Sheet of Twenty 2006

133

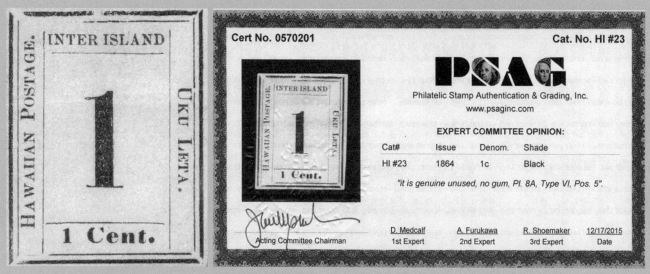

Figure 57: Hawaii Scott # 23, One Cent Black Numerical Stamp. 1864, with SAG Certificate Philatelic Stamp Authentication and grading, Inc. gives Expert Committee Opinion, dated 12/17/2015. It certifies that it is genuine, Plate 8A, Type IV, position 5, (VF-XF) very fine–extra fine condition, unused.

Figure 58: Hawaii Scott # 51 King Kameharmeha IV 1889 known used, cancelled in the postal system, but also received favor cancellations.

You can also use any stamp imagery of your choice. Find a comfortable and relaxing location ... Focus on your breathing. Breathe in and out, calm and relaxed. Gently close your eyes as you drift deeper and deeper into a state of relaxation ... Imagine that you are going to a Euorpean flea market in one of your favorite cities—perhaps London, Paris, or Berlin.

You come across a flea market merchant selling antique stamps, coins, books, clocks, and music boxes. You bargain for an old and interesting book ... You finally get home and begin to open and examine the book, carefully leafing through its pages. Surprised and excited, you discover a beautiful and rare stamp safely stored within the book ...

You wake up from your visual imagery meditation, taking back a feeling of rejuvination and excitement. You are relaxed and rejuvinated in every way.

How did you feel about this visual imagery? _____

What stamp did you discover? _____

What did you do with the stamp? _____

Did you or do you plan to tell anyone about your experience? _____

What was their response? _____

Heart Stamp
Use to connect to the rhythm of your heartbeat.

Select any stamp with an image of a heart (for example, see figure 59).

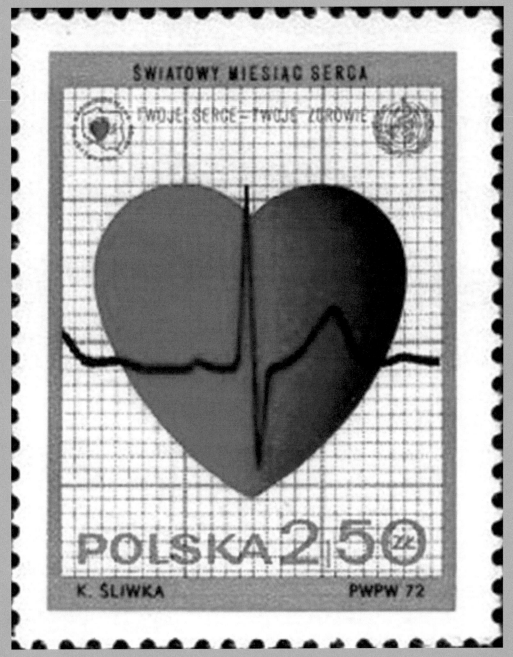

Figure 59: Poland Scott # 1875 World Health Day Heart Medicine, 1972.

With the stamp in your hand, place your hand over your heart to feel your heartbeat. Convert your heartbeat into sound by making a beating vibration with your voice. When this is done, you may gently remove your hand from your heart, but continue to make the beating vibration. Tap your heartbeat on a drum or drum-like surface such as a table, desk, or lap. Continue to tap this rhythm as the sound of your voice stops and the tapping or drumming takes over, becoming the sole vibration that you hear.

You are now connected to your heartbeat and the natural rhythm of your body, the earth, and your surroundings. Enjoy the accepted feeling and therapeutic benefits derived from this exercise. Stop drumming after about five minutes. Your feelings of peace and tranquility will continue after you complete this activity.

8

Special Exercises to Help
Increase Your Life's Balance

Postage stamps are tools for healing and can be used as conduits to understand yourself and others. When these tools are applied to a person, great insights may occur. I have outlined several exercises that will give insights into personalities, behaviors, beliefs, and values.

Birth Year

In this exercise, clients are asked to identify and list stamps that were issued during their birth year and in their birth country. This may be accomplished during a therapy session or completed as an assignment. Prior to the assignment, a brief pretalk should be given to generally inform the person of the history, nature, and uniqueness of postage stamps. Emphasize that one does not have to be a stamp collector to benefit from this therapeutic technique. Stamps may be found by using a stamp catalog or album or by going online. Once the client has made a list of stamps, both client and therapist may discuss how stamps might relate to the client's personality or presenting issues. Such questions may include the following:

1. What did you think and feel about the stamps issued in the year you were born?
2. Were you excited or interested?
3. Were you curious?
4. Do any stamps stand out or have special meaning to you?

5. Do any stamps or topics within the stamps give you clues into your past, present, or future concerns?

Draw a Stamp

Each person is given a sheet of paper, colored pencils, and crayons. They are then asked to draw a postage stamp. No further instructions should be given. When they are done, the client and therapist discuss the drawing. Examples of discussion topics may include the following:

- Discuss your drawing in terms of the size, shape, location on the paper, colors and materials used, choice of topic, amount of postage, perforations, and any other unique characteristics.
- Identify indications in the drawing that connect you to any personal issues, concerns, or plans. Discuss these connections.
- What is the value? Is it rare?
- What is the condition?
- Did you draw an error stamp?

Design a Postage Stamp for Use.

If it is a commemorative stamp, choose the topic and denomination. What is the face value? What does the stamp commemorate? How does this stamp have meaning to you? Discuss in terms of topic, value, and use.

Choose a Stamp

Choose to acquire any stamp in the world. What stamp did you select, and what is the reason for your choice?

Stamp Quiz

Answer the following questions:

1. What country issued the first postage stamp? _____
2. In 1933, what US city was pictured in George Washington's headquarters stamp? _____

3. What is the most valuable stamp in the world? _____

4. What date was the first US postage stamp issued? _____

5. What country pictured President Franklin Roosevelt collecting stamps on a stamp? _____

6. Identify three stamps issued in the year you were born. _____, _____, _____

7. Name six stamp topics. _____, _____, _____, _____,
   _____, _____

8. What year was the first United Nations stamp issued? _____

9. Where was the first United Nations stamp issued? _____

10. Name four fictional heroes on stamps. _____, _____, _____, _____

11. Name three baseball players on stamps. _____, _____, _____

12. Name three Olympic sport participants on stamps. _____, _____, _____

13. Name three movie stars on stamps. _____, _____, _____

CONCLUSION

. . . .

We all want to be balanced. We want to be healthy in body, mind, and spirit. We want happiness, success, accomplishments, confidence, to think clearly, knowledge, positive values, stimulation, purpose, challenges, calmness, and relaxation. With about 7.5–8 billion people on earth, we have more similarities than differences. We can improve our lives by learning from each other. Despite these characteristics, humankind continues to have physical, emotional, and spiritual distress. We often slide into negative behaviors like stress, anxiety, physical illnesses, mental deterioration, and spiritual decline. This book provides a mechanism for eliminating these negative patterns and developing a healing posture in life.

Postage stamps provide powerful healing with a process that enables building better overall health. Additionally, you can super boost this healing power by adding the concepts of hypnosis and self-hypnosis. The hypnosis-stamp process may give you the ability to gain insights into improving your life by connecting you with individuals, groups, and communities throughout the world. Once greater balance begins to dominate your life, a domino effect will take place, growing your confidence, knowledge, character, self-control, clarity, and social relationships.

In this world, we need all of the power, strength, knowledge, and support possible in order to survive. We need strength to push away negativity, disease, and disconnection. This power is especially needed at this time with the world's war and peace status. We are in the midst of the COVID-19 pandemic with all of its medical and political effects—social distancing, educational disruption, and economic business stress. We are also facing world climate change, increased natural disasters, race-relations issues, political-division issues, and gender rights and inequalities. As a result, our balance and wellness are threatened. Stress and anxiety are increasing. Along with this comes increases in alcohol and drug addictions, depression, divorce, job loss, and suicide. We need all the support and help we can get. Let us uncover and use the healing power of postage stamps. You will be glad you did.

AFTERWORD

· ·

The coming together of my two passions in life, social work and philately, have made writing this book a pure pleasure and joy. I neaver dreamed that this would or could ever happen. The more I think about it, the more excited I get. Perhaps I am hypnotized! When the mind and body work together, as exemplified in this book, the potential for growth, change, and healing are limitless. They are infinite. Find your passions in life by using all of your senses, knowledge, and awareness. Your mind affects your body, and your body affects your mind. Your perception may be your reality, and your reality may be your perception. Philately and hypnosis will pave the way and enhance your efforts. Give others and yourself the opportunity to have a lifetime of joy by utilizing the remarkable properties of postage stamps and hypnosis.

About two years ago, and in conjunction with doing research for this book, I attended a large regional stamp show in northern New Jersey. This was the first time I had attended a stamp exhibitition in decades. The visit was a pleasurable, revitalizing experience. While at the show, I stopped at the information booth for the American Topical Association (ATA) and spoke with a representative member who substantiated many of my beliefs in postage stamps. The representative felt that philately was instrumental in his son's admission to medical school. He indicated that during his son's admissions interview, he discussed his interest in stamps, including many of the positive values and characteristics derived from being a collector. One such attribute was attention to detail, which he demonstrated with stamps. The interviewer, also a stamp collector, was impressed. The representative's son was admitted and is now a medical doctor. This is only one of the numerous examples of how stamp collecting may strongly influence your life—perhaps when you least expect it. Have fun and be in good health with stamps. Let the domino effect prevail.

As a testimony to the dynamic healing power of postage stamps, look at the stamp issued in March of 2022, which received immediate world-wide attention. A Russian war ship sent a deadly message to Ukrainian soldiers on land. A Ukrainian soldier immediately responded, "Go fuck yourself." All of this was captured on the March postage stamp. Can you imagine the human power and raw emotions transmitted in this Ukrainian stamp image, which was sent around the world? The warship was later destroyed and sunk by the Ukrainian Army (see figure 60).

Figure 60: Ukraine War Stamp: Russian War Ship Signaling to a Ukrainian Soldier.

I believe that we need stamps now, more than ever. We need stamps, not only for postage services, but for better communication and understanding of who we are as individuals, and as people trying to exist on earth. We need stamps for:

- love,
- kindness,
- peace on earth,
- understanding ourselves and others,
- cooperation,
- communication,
- respect,
- good will toward others,
- helping those in need,
- rewiring our world goals for the better, and
- humanity's advancement.

ADDITIONAL RESOURCES

The American Philatelist Society
American Philatelic Research Library
100 Factory Place
Bellefonte, Pennsylvania 16823
Phone: 814 933-3803
Email: info@stamps.org
www.stamps.org

The American Stamp Dealer and Collector
PO Box 513
Centre Hall, Pennsylvania 16828
Phone: 800 369-8207

American Topical Association
PO Box 2143
Greer, South Carolina 29652
www.ameriacantopicalassn.org

Collectors Club of New York
22 E. 35th Street
New York, New York
Phone: 212 683-0559

Franklin D. Roosevelt Presidential Library and Museum
4079 Albany Post Road
Hyde Park, New York 12538
Phone: 845 486-1140

Hipstamp.com
HipstampMarketplace-Shopping Service

H. R. Harmer
45 Rockefeller Plaza
630 Fifth Avenue Suite 2607
New York, New York 10111
Phone: 929 436-2800
www.hrharmer.com
info@hrharmer.com

Kelleher's Stamp Collectors Quarterly
22 Shelter Rock Lane
Unit 53
Danbury, Connecticut 06810
Phone: 800 212-2830

Linn's Stamp News
PO Box 4129
Sidney, Ohio 45365
Phone: 937 498-0800
www.linns.com

Mystic Stamp Company
9700 Mill Street
Camden, New York 13316
Phone: 800 433-7811
MysticStamp.com

National Guild of Hypnotists
PO Box 308
Merrimack, New Hampshire 03054
Phone: 603 429-9438

National Postal Museum
2 Massachusetts Avenue NE
Washington, DC 20013
www.npm.si.edu

New York State Society for Clinical Social Workers
55 Harrison Road Suite 106
Glen Rock, New Jersey 07452
Phone: 800 288-4279

Scott Catalogue of the United States/Amos Media
1600 Campbell Road Suite A
Sidney, Ohio 45365
Phone: 800 572-6885

Smithsonian National Postal Museum
2 Massachusetts Avenue NE
Washington, DC 20013
www.npm.si.edu

REFERENCES

Amik, George. 1986. *The Inverted Jenny: Money, Mystery, Mania.* Sidney, Ohio: The Amos Press, Inc.

Baltzell, Bob. 2018. *Kellelher's An Amercan Philatelist Franklin Delano Roosevelt.* Danbury, Conneticut: Fourth Quarter.

Bart, Jan, and Phillip Silver. 1965. *Eleanor and Franklin D. Roosevelt Stamps of the World.* American Topical Association, Specialized.

Barron, James. 2017. *The One-Cent Magenta.* Chapel Hill, North Carolina: Algonquin Books of Chapel Hill.

Bigalke, Scott Jay, ed. 2020. *Scott Specialized Catalog of United States Stamps and Covers.* Sidney, Ohio: Amos Media Company.

Blair, Forbes Robbins. 2004. *Instant Self Hypnosis: How to Hypnotize Your-self With Your Eyes Open.* Naperville, Illinois: Sourcebooks, Inc.

Clark, Hugh M., and Theresa M. Clark. 1939. *Scott's Standard Postage Stamp Catalog.* New York: Scott Publications, Inc.

Coogle, David. 2020. *Kelleher's Stamp Collector's Quarterly.* Danbury, Connecticut: 3rd Quarter.

Epting, Charles. 2017. *Design Mistake.* Bellfonte, Pennsylvaina: The American Philatelist Society, Inc.

Greffenhagen, George, and Jerome Husak. 1997. *Adventures in Topical Stamp Collecting*. Canada: Quebecor Printing.

Herst, Herman Jr. 1988. *Nassau Street*. Sidney, Ohio: Amos Press, Inc.

Holland, Paul M. 2020. *The American Philatelist Franklin D. Roosevelt as a Stamp Collector*. Bellfonte, Pennsylvania: The American Philatelist Society, Inc.

Jim, Kahuna Harry Uhane, and Garnette Arledge. 2007. *Wise Secrets of Aloha*. San Francisco: Wiser Books.

Klug, Janet, and Donald J. Sundman. 2007. *100 Greatest American Stamps*. Atlanta, Georgia: Whitman Publishing, LLC.

Lowe, Gary Wayne. 2020. *The American Philatelist*. Bellfonte, Pennsylvania: The American Philatelic Society, Inc.

Marzulla, Elena. 1974. *Pictorial Treasury of US Stamps*. Omaha, Nebraska: Hillman Graphics Company.

Mottin, Donald J. 2005, *Raising Your Children With Hypnosis,* Bridgeton, Missouri: ASC HypnoClassics.

Nathan, M. C., and W. S. Boggs. 1962. *The Pony Express*. New York: The Collectors Club.

Perlmutter, Austin, and David Perlmutter. 2020. *Brain Wash*. New York: Hachett Book Group.

Pettit, Ted S., ed. 1948. *Handbook for Boys*. New Brunswick, New Jersey: Boy Scouts of America.

Rossi, Ernest Lawrence. 1993. *The Psychology of Mind-Body Healing: New Concepts of Therapeutic Hypnosis*. New York: W. W. Norton and Company, Inc.

Schwartz, Andrew E. 1995. *Guided Imagery for Groups*. Duluth, Minnesota: Whole Person Associates, Inc.

Snee, Charles. 2013. *Scott 2014 Specialized Catalog of United States Stamps and Covers*. Sidney, Ohio: Scott Publishing Company.

Sundman, Donald. 2020. *Mystic's 2020 US Stamp Catalog*. Vol. 2. Camden, New York: Mystic Stamp Company.

Sundman, Donald. 2020. *Mystic's 2020 US Stamp Catalog*. Vol. 5. Camden, New York: Mystic Stamp Company.

Toth, George. 2014. *Seashell Therapy*. Bloomington, Indiana: iUniverse.

Weill, Andrew. 1995. *Spontaneous Healing*. New York: Ballantine Books.

Williams, Harley. 1952. *The Conquest of Fear*. Oxford: The Alden Press.

Youngblood, Wayne L. 2019. *The American Stamp Dealer and Collector*. Leesport, Pennsylvania: The American Stamp Dealer's Association, Inc.

Zimberoff, Diane. 2004. *Hypnotherapy Training*. Issaquah, Washington: The Wellness Institute Heart-Centered Therapies.